BACK TO BAINBRIDGE

NORAH LALLY

Abbey Glen Press

Copyright © 2024 by Norah Lally
All rights reserved.

No part of this publication may be reproduced, distributed, or transmitted in any form or by any means, including photocopying, recording, or other electronic or mechanical methods, without the prior written permission of the publisher, except as permitted by U.S. copyright law. For permission requests, contact abbeyglenpress.com.

This is a work of fiction. Names, characters, places and incidents either are the product of the author's imagination or are used fictitiously. No identification with actual persons (living or deceased), is intended or should be inferred.

ISBN 978-1-64704-872-3 (paperback)
ISBN 978-1-64704-873-0 (hardcover)
ISBN 978-1-64704-874-7 (ebook)
ISBN 978-1-64704-875-4 (audiobook)

Visit the author online at norahlally.com

Dedicated to the memory of my beloved grandmothers:

Kitty Lane, who left a farm in Limerick and made the Bronx her home;

and Helen McGinnis, who quietly longed to know her father.

CHAPTER 1

I RAN UPSTAIRS two steps at a time, took a second to look around my empty room, then walked over to my closet. Inside, near the back, I pulled up a loose floorboard. From the hole underneath, I retrieved my prized items: a plastic wallet shaped like a ladybug, the first-place synchronized swimming ribbon I'd won last summer at the rec center, and the souvenir family photo taken the day we all went apple picking for my eighth birthday. In the picture, I'm standing with my arms wrapped around my little sister and brother. Both my parents are holding apples on top of their heads and grinning like nothing's wrong. *Fakers.*

Mom called from outside: "Hurry up and get your butt in the car, Vic!" She sounded exasperated, as usual. "You trying to get me arrested? We're not supposed to be here!"

I stuffed the ribbon in my pocket, the wallet and photo in my backpack, then ran downstairs and out the front door. My sister and brother, Judith and Dylan, were already in the backseat. All my family's worldly possessions—packed haphazardly in suitcases, backpacks, and black trash bags—were stuffed into the minivan up to its ceiling. I climbed into the passenger seat and slammed the door.

"Watch your feet," Mom scolded. I looked down and noticed my feet were resting on her scuffed magenta suitcase.

"Where'm I supposed to put my feet?" I asked.

"Just not on my stuff, please." She started the car and put it into gear.

"It's just a stupid suitcase," I scoffed.

"It's not. It's very important to me," Mom said, her eyes welling up with tears.

I hated when she cried. She backed out of the driveway.

"What's so important in there?" I asked.

"Nothing's '*so*' important. Nothing that's any of your business, anyway," she snapped.

Whenever Mom said something was none of my business, it made me wonder. A feeling in my stomach told me I should probably make it my business.

As we pulled away, I watched our house get smaller and smaller in the minivan's side mirror. I shoved my fists in my pockets, then extended both hidden middle fingers. I wasn't even sure exactly who I was flipping off. Probably

Mom. Or the landlord. Or the sheriff who'd told us we had to leave. Or everyone in Middleton, for being jerks and having houses their families could afford.

It was dusk on a hot July night. Streetlights came on as we pulled onto the main road. I was sweaty. The backs of my thighs stuck to the car seat.

"Are we going to Grandma's?" asked Judith, nervously twirling her hair.

"Grandma didn't pick up," Mom said, her jaw tight.

"Why not?" I asked.

"How should I know, Vicki?"

Mom usually took her frustrations out on me. Probably because I was the oldest kid. Like it was somehow my fault that she lost her job, we got evicted, Grandma hated us, and we had nowhere to go.

"Guess we're officially camping in our car then," I sighed.

"Don't say that," said Mom. "Just be quiet for a minute so I can think."

Inside my pocket, I fingered the silky fabric of my synchro ribbon. I'd won it only a week earlier. My first win. And probably my last.

Mom had signed all three of us up for day camp at the rec center so she could look for a job. I got placed on the synchronized swim squad because it was the only activity that wasn't already filled up. Coach Marissa put me in a trio group with two girls named Brianna and Emily. The three of us instantly made a connection, hanging out at the town pool together after practices, eating fries and popsicles from the snack bar, and making TikToks on Brianna's phone. In the county-wide competition, we placed first in the 13/14 age category for our routine. That's where the ribbon came from.

Having friends, being a winner. Nice while it lasted. Now we were moving again, for the sixth time in five years. Middleton had been our home for exactly six months. We moved there after Mom had gotten dumped by Stan, her latest in a string of bad boyfriends. Mom always joked that her picker was broken when it came to men. It wasn't funny.

"Vic, you want some?" Dylan's grubby hand reached up from the back seat. He was ten years old but usually acted about five, always carrying his teddy bear around like a baby.

I inspected the offering. A crumbly corner of an overly handled Pop-Tart. "No thanks, Dyl. You go ahead and finish it."

"Too gross," muttered Judith. She was twelve, but tried to act older. "*So* not okay."

A few minutes later, Mom pulled into the parking lot of the motel by the freeway. I studied the license plate of the car in front of us and said the letters and numbers in my head. K39 2CJ. It was a thing I did.

A little bird with a puffy orange chest sat perched on a trash can at the edge of the parking lot. It cocked its head and peered straight at me. Can a bird have a facial expression? This one came across as very judgy. Like it had never seen a raggedy-ass family with all their crap loaded into their minivan before. Like it could tell I was reciting a dumb license plate in my head, and it wasn't a bit impressed.

In the motel lobby, two guys in matching jumpsuits were changing the sign on the wall from *Comfort Inn* to *Quality Inn & Suites*. The lady at the front desk had clumpy mascara and a badge pinned to her blouse that said, 'My Name is Cookie.'

"I apologize for the construction, ma'am," she said robotically when Mom approached the desk. Her face stretched into a waxy smile. "We're in transition at the moment."

"So are we, Cookie," Mom chuckled. She opened her purse.

I looked down and focused all the intensity of my energy into tracing the faux woodgrain of the floor with my eyes. It was like a highway. To where …? No matter. I'd have taken that road any place it led. I pressed my fingernails into the palms of my sweaty hands and prayed Mom's card wouldn't be declined. I had a hundred and eight dollars in my ladybug wallet, just in case. But I had other plans for that.

CHAPTER 2

After the blackout curtains were closed and the lights were flicked off in our motel room that night, I stared into the darkness and tried to recall the license plate I'd seen in the parking lot. K39 something. The hotel pillow beneath my head was mushy, and it smelled like a combination of bleach and lavender.

I was supposed to be hanging with my friends, getting excited to start high school in the fall. But instead, I was with Mom, Judith, and Dylan bumping around aimlessly again. Leaving town abruptly had become a bad habit since my dad had disappeared six years earlier. Mom never quite managed to land us on our feet in any of the places we'd tried to settle down. It stressed me out. I hated having to keep trying to make new friends and fit in over and over again every time I started at a different school.

If only Dad had stayed, everything would be closer to normal, I thought as I lay awake.

Truth is, I thought about him a lot, and often thought about running away and searching for him. Not too long after my eighth birthday, the day we had gone apple picking, a sound woke me up late one night. I got up from my bed and tiptoed to the kitchen. Out the window, I saw my dad throw his brown leather duffel bag into his Ford truck. Then I watched him drive off, my eyes fixed on the license plate until it was so far away that I couldn't make it out. X35 101.

Mom cursed and cried when she realized he had left us. She said he ran off with Janice, the lady from the diner who wore bells on her boots. She said Dad was a bum and a liar and a deadbeat and a lowlife. She said he left us high and dry.

My dad only called once after that, about a month later. I picked up the phone. He told me he missed me, Judith, and Dylan. He told me he had made it across the country to a beautiful town called Oh-hi. A magical place with pink sunsets, glorious mountains, miles of orange groves, horses, and ice cream parlors. He promised he'd send for us to come visit him soon.

But we never heard from him again after that.

I blamed Mom. She changed her phone number when we moved. And whenever I asked about Dad, she got angry. So, I eventually stopped bringing him up. But I became an expert on Oh-hi. It took me a while to realize it was actually spelled O-j-a-i. I googled it regularly, pulling up images of local events to see if I could spot my father. There were lots of yoga studios and art galleries and breath coaches and sound baths. California things.

Maybe my dad had become a spiritual guru, or maybe he was pumping gas. I didn't care which; I just really wanted to see him again, and find out why he had left us. I wondered if Mom might've done something to drive him away. Her grouchy attitude always seemed to ruin everything.

The hundred and eight dollars I'd saved from babysitting and birthdays and odd jobs wasn't quite enough to buy a train ticket across the country, but it was close. I had looked up fares on Amtrak.com.

At some point, I must've finally fallen asleep in that weird Comfort/Quality Inn bed, because the next morning I woke to the *tip-tip-tip-tip-tip* sound of gentle raindrops pattering on the metal air conditioning unit outside the window, and the *whooooshing* of traffic on the freeway about fifty yards away. If I imagined hard enough, the traffic noise could almost be an ocean breeze. I pictured myself standing in soft sand on the Pacific coast, about to begin an epic day in which I'd get to drink out of a coconut and try jet-skiing for the first time.

As my eyes adjusted to the morning light, I took in the motel room with its two queen beds, maroon carpeting, small round table, hardback wooden chairs, TV, microwave, and mini fridge. Judith lay beside me in the bed closest to the window. She was asleep with a furrowed brow, grinding her teeth. Although she was two years younger, Judith was just as big as I was and took up three-quarters of the bed with her legs and arms sprawled out. I, on the other hand, was small for my age, skinny with no figure to speak of. A 'late bloomer,' Mom called me.

In the other bed, Mom and Dylan were curled up together, breathing in unison as if dreaming the same dream. Mr. Choofie, Dylan's teddy bear, had dropped onto the carpet in an awkward lump.

I got up and tiptoed over to the window, moving the curtain aside slightly. There was a chubby little bird with an orange breast perched on the ledge outside, peering right into the window at me. It looked like the same one from the parking lot yesterday.

"Are you following me, you little lunatic?" I whispered, flicking at the plexiglass with my index finger. It flew away. Never to be seen again, most likely. Good riddance.

An hour later, Mom finally got ahold of Grandma and slipped into the bathroom to talk in private, running the water so we couldn't eavesdrop. When she came out, her expression was a combination of relieved and rageful—not an easy look to pull off. But Mom was a pro at looks like that. Complicated emotions were kind of her *thing*.

"Get your stuff together, kids," she chirped. "We're going to Grandma's!"

On our way out of town, we drove past the rec center pool where I'd learned to do a ballet leg, crane and flamingo positions, and underwater eggbeaters until my leg muscles burned and cramped. I hadn't minded the pain, though. It was worth it. I felt a tear and rubbed it out of my eye before anyone could see it.

Goodbye, Middleton. Goodbye, proud wooden houses behind neatly trimmed shrubbery. Goodbye, grocery store, train station, post office, and 7-11. The cars were driving too fast for me to catch any of their license plate numbers. Which, of course, did not bode well. Not at all.

But leaving Middleton was only part of the problem. The real issue was where we were headed. Going to Grandma's pretty much meant we were at the end of the line in terms of desperation. It was common knowledge that Mom and Grandma lowkey couldn't stand each other. Usually when they got together, they ended up having a fight and then not speaking for months. The thought of us all crammed together in her small apartment made me shudder.

"We'll probably just hang at Grandma's through the summer," Mom said, as if reading my thoughts. "This isn't permanent." She merged onto Interstate 87 toward NYC.

"Just until I find a job and we get another place of our own."

"Don't worry, Mr. Choofie," said Dylan, pressing his bear's face up to the window, "Grandma's house will be fun."

"*So* frickin' fun," I grumbled.

"Don't you start, Vicki," Mom warned. "We're all coping the best we can."

The route took us past a bunch of little towns lining the Hudson River, then across a bridge and down the highway through Westchester County. Leafy shrubbery on either side of the road gradually gave way to modest two-family houses with aluminum siding, followed by Yonkers Raceway, industrial buildings, and finally, the "Welcome to the Bronx" sign.

We exited at Mosholu Parkway, and a few minutes later turned onto Bainbridge Avenue. The minivan's blinker clicked apprehensively.

"Mr. Choofie says he misses Middleton," announced Dylan, his voice shaky.

"Not me," said Judith. "All the kids there were so douchey."

"What's *dooshy* again?" asked Dylan.

"Never mind, Dyl."

Mom slowed down as she drove up the block looking for a parking spot. Groups of people were always hanging out on the sidewalk and stoops of Grandma's neighborhood. Laughter and music with a big bouncy beat came from somewhere up the street, and a rap track with a rattling bassline boomed from a passing car's window, shaking our seats. Unfamiliar spicy smells hit my nostrils.

A gold car with tinted windows pulled away from the curb right in front of Grandma's building. I noted its license plate and said it silently in a syncopated rhythm: XJC 971.

"The parking gods have surely shone down upon us," Mom crowed. "This practically never happens. It's a very good omen." After three tries, she successfully parallel parked and then pulled the keys out of the ignition, turning to face us.

"Promise me you'll behave yourselves. All three of you."

We nodded solemnly. *But really, Mom: When has that ever happened?*

CHAPTER 3

The apartment building's front door was propped open with a bucket. Inside, a man was busy cleaning the handrails along the staircase, a rag in one hand and a spray bottle in the other.

"Excuse us," Mom said, politely.

The man looked up from his work. His eyes scanned Mom, Judith, Dylan, and me, standing at the base of the staircase with all our bags.

"Can I help you?" he asked. His voice was friendly enough, but slightly territorial.

"I'm Susan Hanlon. My mother is Ellen Casey, up in 4D?" Mom had her magenta suitcase in one hand, and a silly-looking straw tote bag in the other, as if she was coming directly from a beach vacation. By then I was itching to find out what was in that magenta suitcase. It was too small to hold her clothes. It had to be something else. Keepsakes? Important documents? Clues about what happened to Dad?

The man moved aside so we could ascend the stairs. "Will you *all* be staying with Mrs. Casey?" he asked as Mom squeezed past him with a pursed smile.

"Only for a little while," she said reassuringly. "Just visiting. Are you the new super?"

"Not new," he said. "I've been here two years."

It had been a while since we'd visited Grandma.

"The hallways look great," Mom commented.

The man smiled broadly from behind his bushy mustache. "This building is the cleanest on the block now," he boasted.

I looked away. Flirty Mom was even more unbearable than cranky Mom or weepy Mom. I checked the man's hand for a wedding ring. He was wearing one.

"Can we pick up the pace?" I asked, irritated. "I have to pee."

I ushered Mom up the stairs.

"Anything you need while you're visiting, you let me know, Susan," the super said. "Name's Ernesto."

We were all panting by the time we reached the fourth floor, the top level of the building. Mom walked to the door marked 4D and pressed the little, round, black button in the center. It made a harsh buzzing sound, like an angry wasp.

I couldn't help noticing that the buzzer button resembled a Junior Mint candy. My stomach churned. We hadn't eaten anything all day except for some snack mix hours before, from the vending machine at the motel.

A shuffling sound came from the other side of the door.

"Who's there?" barked Grandma's voice.

Mom answered, "It's us, Ma!"

There was a good ten seconds of clicking and clacking, twisting and pulling on the other side of the door as Grandma dealt with a series of deadbolts and chain locks. Then the door opened.

The first words out of Grandma's mouth were, "How on earth did you get in the building? I didn't buzz you in."

"Nice to see you, too, Ma," Mom said.

Grandma wore a T-shirt picturing a floppy-eared hound dog in a bed of daisies. Her curly brown hair had gray strands and was cut short, framing her round face. Her gray-blue eyes were the same shape and shade as mine, but they looked oversized and owly behind thick, round glasses. She leaned her pudgy arm on the doorframe, barring our entrance.

"The sight of the lot of you," Grandma murmured, shaking her head. Then she opened the door wide and stepped back, gesturing us inside. "Well, get your butts in, before the neighbors start making up their stories."

"Oh, please," said Mom. "What stories could they possibly make up, Ma?"

We filed into the apartment, and Grandma shut and re-locked the door behind us.

"The neighbors love to gossip. You should know that by now, Susan," she continued.

"And *you* should know by now that I don't give a dang," Mom retorted, making her way down the narrow hallway toward the living room.

I followed Mom. The apartment smelled good, of cinnamon and perfume. There were three doors off the narrow hallway. The first door led to a small bedroom, the second was the bathroom, and the third was the kitchen. At the end of the hallway was the living room, with two large windows looking out onto Bainbridge Avenue. Then, on the other side of the living room was the door leading to Grandma's room, which was off-limits. I'd only been in there once before, when I had snuck in years earlier during one of our rare visits. I remembered trying to escape from the sounds of my mother and grandmother arguing over whether or not baby Dylan would be baptized in church. Their desperate, prickly voices frightened me. But it suddenly got nice and quiet once I climbed inside Grandma's big mahogany wardrobe. No yelling. No aching and rage bubbling just under the surface. My grandmother's neatly hanging dresses and sweaters muffled the sounds of the outside world, and the mothball scent was, strangely, a comfort. I felt so safe and warm curled up in there, somehow, even though it was dark and more than a little spooky. When Mom finally found me after frantically searching for half an hour, I'll never forget the harsh scolding I had to endure the whole drive home, for wandering off and entering a space in which I didn't belong and wasn't allowed.

Now, Mom put her suitcase and straw bag in the corner of the living room next to the television, and we added our bags beside them to make a small, pathetic pile. A local news program was on the TV. There were doilies on the coffee table and saint statues on the doilies. Grandma worked as the administrator of the parish office at nearby St. Brendan's Church, and she was really into God stuff. Mom had once told me that she'd had religion shoved down her throat when she was a kid, and then she grew up and realized it's all a load of garbage.

"Ernesto really shouldn't leave the front door open," Grandma said in an irritated tone. "Lord knows who might wander in."

"He seemed nice," Mom remarked.

Grandma grunted. "Of course he's nice," she said. "He wants tips."

Then she turned to face me. "Let me have a look at my grandkids," she continued. "It's been forever since I last saw you."

We stood in a line awkwardly, awaiting inspection.

"You're still a twig, Victoria," she said.

"I prefer to call her the human string bean," Judith laughed.

"And what're you my dear, a hyena?" Grandma asked, frowning.

Judith shut up quick. Dylan hugged Mr. Choofie tight.

Nothing got by Grandma. Like a hawk spotting prey, she trained her sight on her grandson. "Still with that bear, I see," she said in a disapproving tone. "How old are you now, young man?"

"He's ten, Ma. You know that," said Mom.

Grandma did the sign of the cross and looked at the sky.

"Leave him, Ma," Mom insisted, her volume and agitation rising.

Grandma rolled her eyes and gestured toward our heap of bags in the corner.

"You brought a lot of things," she commented.

"Oh, there's way more in the car," Judith said. Mom shot her a look.

"Don't worry," Mom said quickly. "We can put some of it away in the basement. You still have storage space down there, don't you?"

"Yes," Grandma replied. "Ernesto has the key. We'll get him to carry a load down there tomorrow."

"Mr. Choofie says he's absolutely famished," Dylan squeaked.

"Sweet vocab word, Dyl," Judith scoffed.

"Dear heavens," said Grandma, looking upward as if talking to God himself. "The bear is hungry. Give me strength. I'll go make some sandwiches."

She went to the kitchen, leaving us alone in the living room. There was a collective sigh of relief. On the television, an anchorwoman in a low-cut blouse was describing a subway flasher on the loose who'd been busy showing commuters his privates.

"I'm not in the mood for stories about sickos right now," Mom said. She grabbed the remote off the table and shut off the TV. "Why don't you kids go unpack your things in the bedroom down the hall?"

My heart stopped as the realization of what Mom said sunk in. "*The* bedroom down the hall? Wait, I'm not sleeping in the same room with Judith and Dylan, am I?"

"It's a two-bedroom apartment, Vic," she said, enunciating slowly as if I was stupid. "Do the math. Grandma has her room, you three kids will be in the other, and I'll camp out here in the living room."

"But, Mom," I protested, "I *can't* be with them. I'm older now. I need my privacy."

"I'm in my thirties, and look where I'm sleeping." Mom pointed toward the lumpy old couch.

I grabbed my backpack and walked angrily down the hall. "Maybe you shouldn't have gotten fired from your job then," I said under my breath as I walked away.

"What did you just say?" Mom called. But I kept walking.

"Give her some time alone," I heard Dylan say to Mom. "She's being a teen."

The rooms at Grandma's were simple and tidy. The walls were bare, except for a porcelain cross hanging in the hallway with a little protruding bowl containing holy water. Holy water is water that's been blessed by a priest. I knew that because last time we were visiting, Grandma showed me the gallon jugs of it that she kept in the closet that she'd had blessed at the church where she worked. Enough to last a lifetime.

The bedroom I was to share with Judith and Dylan was decent-sized but oddly shaped, with five corners of varying acute angles. Sparsely decorated with one dresser and—to my horror—only one full size bed with a trundle underneath. There was a single narrow window in the room. I walked over to it and pulled back the lace curtain. It looked out onto an airshaft, which meant the view was of a brick wall, with other people's apartment windows only a couple feet away. A pigeon was perched on the opposite sill.

"What is it with you birds lately?" I asked. "Always in my business. Shoo!" The pigeon let out a soft coo that came from somewhere deep inside its little bird body, then turned and flapped its way up the narrow airshaft toward the sky.

I unzipped my backpack and checked to make sure my photograph and ladybug wallet were still in the small interior pouch. Then I methodically took my socks and underwear out of my bag. I laid claim to the top two drawers in the dresser, transferring my things there. My prized possessions, I decided, would go underneath my clothing in the top drawer. I pulled the synchro ribbon out of my pocket and placed it there. Then I lingered for a moment to study the apple-picking photo for the zillionth time.

"Come eat!" I heard Grandma call from the kitchen.

I shoved the photo to the back of the drawer, too, then covered all my things with clothing and shut the drawer firmly.

Judith and Dylan were already seated at the small kitchen table when I walked in.

"Put those sandwiches down!" Grandma scolded. They froze mid-bite.

"You will wait until I'm seated, and we've thanked God for our food," Grandma ordered.

I sat down on one of the empty chairs. Mom's was empty.

"She has a migraine," said Judith, off my look.

That meant Mom took a pill, and she would be out cold for the next couple hours.

Grandma sat down and looked expectantly around the table at us.

"Did your mother never teach you to place your napkins on your laps?" she asked.

Grandma unfolded her paper napkin and smoothed it across her thighs. We did the same. Grandma clasped her hands together. We mimicked her movements as if we were playing a mirroring game.

She cleared her throat as though about to make an official proclamation.

"Dear Lord," she said, "we thank you for your bounty. We pray you bless this table and this family. That our sacrifices may be worthy and that we may someday be at peace in your kingdom in heaven. Amen."

Grandma opened one eye. It was aimed straight at me like a laser. Creepy.

"Amen," I said. I kicked Judith under the table.

"Ow!" yelped Judith. "Aaaaaaaaa - to the - MEN!"

"What kind of kingdom is it in heaven?" asked Dylan. "Do they have unicorns?"

Grandma's eyes narrowed. But she picked up her sandwich. Finally, we all started eating.

Turkey slices and cheese with lettuce and mustard, and pickle slices on the side.

I wouldn't have admitted it out loud because I wouldn't have wanted to give my mean old Grandma the satisfaction, but it was the tastiest meal I'd had in as long as I could remember.

CHAPTER 4

THERE WAS A lot to get used to about being under Grandma's roof. For starters, all the rules and chores. Mom, for all her faults, had a few qualities I appreciated. One of them was she wasn't strict about keeping everything neat. She was chill about stuff like that. But Grandma was a tyrant when it came to housekeeping. We had barely settled in that first day when she made Judith wash dishes, and shoved a stack of linens into my arms, ordering me to make up the bed and trundle in our bedroom.

It's embarrassing to admit, but before then I don't think I had ever made a bed in my life. What I learned was that getting the elastic to stay on one corner of the mattress while you stretch the sheet all the way to the other side requires an amazing amount of strength and dexterity. Once I finally wrestled the sheets on so they'd stay, I yanked the bedspread up, smoothed it out to the best of my ability, and then sprawled out on top of my masterpiece, completely spent by the effort.

After that exhausting battle, I hardly had an instant of rest before Grandma bustled in and spent the next five minutes pointing out the many ways in which my bed-making techniques sucked. Judith's dishwashing was all wrong too.

While we were both redoing our chores to Grandma's satisfaction, she dragged a yelping Dylan into the bathroom to cut his hair, even though he wanted to grow it long and Mom had said he could. Since Mom was passed out on the couch, she couldn't very well stand up to Grandma about any of this extreme unfairness.

A few minutes later, Dylan shuffled into the bedroom with red eyes and a runny nose. I couldn't help but gasp. With his hair trimmed neatly, he looked years older. Like a regular ten-year-old. Eleven, even.

"She actually did an awesome job, Dyl," I said.

Judith, putting her clothes away in the empty bottom drawers of the dresser, looked up at him too.

"Wow, you do look good," she agreed, before remembering to be sarcastic. "... for a booger-eater," she added.

Dylan gave a forlorn shrug and a loud sniffle.

"We're using all the drawers, so you'll have to keep your clothes in the closet, sniffly McSniffinstein," I told him.

He walked over to the closet, opened the door, and went inside. Judith tiptoed over and shut the door, giggling.

"Nighty night!" she called, trapping him.

"Leave it open a crack, you buttface!" Dylan roared from inside.

I covered my ears as the screaming cuss words began to fly. That's when I realized once again what a nightmare it was going to be to share a room with these two.

Grandma suddenly appeared in the doorway.

"Pipe down!" she growled, pulling Judith away from the closet and opening the door to free Dylan. "If you children make a racket, Miss Kirby downstairs will come after you."

On cue, the floor started vibrating, and there was a loud banging sound. *Bam, bam, bam! Bam, bam, bam!*

"What's that?" Dylan asked.

"Kirby hitting her ceiling with a broom handle. You don't want to be on her bad side."

"What a psycho!" said Judith.

"You don't know the half of it," Grandma said. "That old woman is mean as a snake, and doesn't like children one little bit. She makes me look like Glinda the Good Witch."

Bam, Bam, Bam, Bam, Bam!

Dylan froze, his eyes widening at the thought of a wicked witch living downstairs.

"I don't want to meet her," he whispered.

"You better behave then," Grandma said, wagging a finger at him.

We stayed very quiet for the rest of the evening. After we'd brushed our teeth, changed into our PJs, and passed Grandma's inspection on both counts, Mom finally rose from the living room couch like a creature from a lost lagoon. She came into our bedroom, her cheek creased with an imprint from one of the embroidered sofa pillows. I climbed into bed next to Judith, and Dylan slipped under the covers on his trundle below.

"Ah … It's nice and neat in here," Mom said, vaguely looking around. "Good job putting your stuff away, kiddos."

"There's a mean old lady living downstairs, you know," said Dylan, sitting upright in his trundle bed.

"Yup, she's been here a hundred years," said Mom knowingly. "Miss Kirby. Rarely comes out of her apartment. But if you annoy her, she might put a hex on you or something. So, watch it."

"Whatever," scoffed Judith. "I'm not afraid."

"Good," shrugged Mom. "That seals it then. You'll be the first one she stirs into her soup." She tickled Judith, who giggled like a toddler.

Dylan wasn't laughing, though. "I'm really scared, Mom," he said.

I swatted him with my pillow. "Get a grip, Dyl. There's no such thing as witches. But if Miss Kirby hears you, she'll start banging again."

Mom walked in a circle around the little bedroom as if in a trance, running her hand over the wooden dresser as she passed it.

"This used to be my room," she mused with a faraway look in her eyes. She sat on the corner of the bed and looked up at the ceiling. I followed her gaze and noticed a few dead bugs inside the frosted glass bowl covering the lightbulb overhead. I also spotted a strand of hair trapped under layers of paint in the decorative molding where the wall met the ceiling. It had probably been painted over about twenty times or more, I figured, throughout the course of years and years. It could've been a hair from a paintbrush, or maybe even from Mom's own head, back when she was young and had slept in this very bed.

"I couldn't *wait* to get out of here," Mom sighed, smoothing out the bedspread. "I jumped at my first opportunity: your father. And we all know how *that* turned out."

It always annoyed me when Mom acted all regretful and victimy about Dad; like her life would've been *so* much better if she had never met him. What about me, Judith, and Dylan? We wouldn't have existed it they hadn't met. And yes, he abandoned us, but at least *some* of the blame for that had to be hers, too, right? After all, *she* was the one with the broken picker. What else had she done to make him leave?

Mom cleared her throat. "Things will be better from now on," she declared, in a strained voice that I think was meant to sound hopeful. A C-minus performance at best.

"How do you know will things be better, Mom?" Dylan asked.

"Because they can't get any worse," she said, and flicked off the light.

CHAPTER 5

JUDITH'S TEETH GRINDING issue meant that she was the worst bedmate ever. That first night at Grandma's I went through an avalanche of license plates in my mind, trying to block out the nails-on-a-chalkboard sound of her molars scraping the enamel off themselves, which was next-level disturbing. Every time I started to relax, my eyes would suddenly pop open and I'd have to reorient myself to the room we were in. There were faint sounds I could hear through the airshaft window: water rushing out of a faucet, the clinking of dishes, a baby crying, a faraway siren, high-pitched laughter.

Even the weight of the air felt different on Bainbridge Avenue. Everyone was so tightly packed in: two girls in my bed, three kids in our room, four rooms in the apartment, four apartments per floor, six floors per building, twenty buildings per block. That's a lot of people in close proximity, I thought, all inhaling oxygen and exhaling carbon dioxide. This was the kind of stuff I obsessed over while other people slept. I sat up to catch my breath, feeling claustrophobic, listening to the muffled sounds in the shrouded stillness.

That's when a singular voice started to emerge among the noises echoing through the airshaft.

"I know you, I walked with you once upon a dream..."

I instantly recognized the song as one that Princess Aurora sang in *Sleeping Beauty*. I must've watched that movie a hundred times back when I was a little kid. I scooted to the foot of the bed, taking special care not to wake Judith, reached my toes down to the rag rug covering the wood floor, and tiptoed over to the window, putting my ear to it.

"I know you, the gleam in your eyes is so familiar a gleam..."

It was a girl's voice.

"Yet I know it's true that visions are seldom all they seem..."

Pressing my forehead to the window screen, I peered out into the airshaft. Neighbors' windows looked back at me. Some lighted, some dark. I couldn't tell where the voice was coming from.

"But if I know you, I know what you'll do..."

As quietly as possible, I twisted the latch to pull the screen open so I could get a better look. The metal frame of the screen squeaked a teensy bit, and the singing immediately stopped.

"Hello?" the voice called up through the humid darkness. "Is somebody there?"

Quickly, I crouched down on the floor beneath the windowsill and held my breath. Judith made a terrible scraping noise with her molars but didn't wake up.

After a moment the singing started again.

"You'll love me at once, the way you did once upon a dream ..."

I pulled myself up and poked my head out the window. Looked down. The voice was definitely coming from the first or second floor.

Trying to get a clearer view, I shifted my weight and my elbow accidentally knocked over a little plastic saint statue that was sitting on the inside window ledge. And out it tumbled, falling fast with hands together in prayer, ricocheting down the airshaft with a hollow clattering sound. The singing stopped again. I bit my bottom lip hard and leaned back inside. Screw Grandma's dumb religious figurines all over the place!

"Who's that?" called the girl's voice, in a firm and steady tone. "I know you're up there. Come on, show your face!"

Reluctantly, I stuck my head out the window. "Hey there," I said, keeping my voice to a whisper so as not to wake up Judith and Dylan. In the shadows, I could make out the form of a girl crouched on her first-floor windowsill.

"Who are you?" the mysterious girl asked.

"Vicki," I said into the musky air. "And I swear, I'm not a stalker or anything. I just wanted to see who was singing." I spoke as quietly as I could, so as not to tempt the wrath of Miss Kirby one flight below me. But the airshaft intensified every sound.

"You're one of Mrs. Casey's grandkids?" the girl asked.

"How'd you know?"

She looked up toward me, swinging her legs out the first story window. I could see she had long black hair and shiny hoop earrings.

"For one thing, you're up in 4D. For another thing, my pops met you earlier. He's the super," she explained.

"Oh. Hi."

"What was that thing that fell?"

"One of my grandma's little saint statues."

"Oooh. How sacrilegious."

"I knocked it over by accident," I said. "I didn't mean any disrespect."

The girl giggled. "I'm just messin' with you. It's a piece of plastic. I highly doubt God cares about that kind of thing. He—or she—is probably pretty busy with more important stuff."

She hopped out her window and stood on the ground at the bottom of the airshaft, searching by her feet, which were clad in black sneakers.

"Sorry if I bothered you," she said, kicking around with the toe of her sneaker. "I like to sing in the airshaft because there's good reverb."

I had no idea what that meant, but didn't feel like asking, in case it was something I should know. Every time we plopped down in a new neighborhood, there were always expressions and styles that I had to pick up fast. I was pretty good at the art of pretending to know what was going on when I was clueless.

"You didn't bother me at all," I said. "I liked your singing."

The girl bent down and then rose, triumphant, with the statuette in her hand. She inspected it.

"Ohhhhh! It's the Virgin Mary," she said. "Why didn't you say so? She's kind of a big deal."

"My bad," I apologized.

"Catch!" she said suddenly, tossing the little Mary skyward with all her might. But it fell short of the fourth floor window and hit the ground again.

She made two more attempts, unsuccessful. By then we were both stifling laughter, because the poor little holy Mary was being abused so unceremoniously.

"I suck at throwing," she finally conceded. "How about we meet up on the front stoop in the morning, and I'll give you back your grandma's Mary."

"Okay. What time?"

"Ten?"

The girl climbed back into her window and started to close the screen.

"Wait—" I said. "What's your name?"

"Rosa," she said. "Rosa Rodriguez." And in that instant, a light went on in another window somewhere on another floor, throwing a beam of yellow across the airshaft that illuminated Rosa's face. I could see that she was about my age, and I sensed an achy feeling somewhere deep inside that resembled hopefulness, like back when I had my synchro trio. Friendship. I longed for it. But I didn't want to get ahead of myself.

"Bye," I whispered into the night air.

Rosa disappeared inside her apartment again. I shut the window screen with another annoying squeak. Dylan made a little groaning sound.

"Shhhh. It's okay," I whispered, bending down to the trundle to readjust my little brother's blanket around him and Mr. Choofie. "Everything's okay."

Gingerly climbing back into bed beside Judith, I was much too excited to be tired. I reached under my pillow for my phone. Yes, I realized I was frying my mind with electromagnetic waves as I slept. I was ok with living dangerously. Turning the screen toward the wall so the glow didn't wake Judith, I deleted Middleton, NY as my default location, changing it to Bronx, NY. I scrolled over to the weather app and noted that the next day would be hazy with a high of eighty-nine. In Ojai, my other preset location, they were expecting clear skies and temperatures in the mid-seventies.

CHAPTER 6

I WOKE UP at eight in the morning and went to the bathroom. To my surprise, Mom was in there looking at herself in the mirror above the sink, putting on lipstick. Mom normally slept late and hardly ever wore lipstick. But on that morning, she wore a clean, not-too-wrinkly button-down shirt and her best jeans, and she had ironed her hair straight, which she usually only did if she had a date.

"What are you doing, Mom?" I asked.

"Gonna go look for a job," she said.

"Already?" I was surprised.

"No time like the present!" Mom pressed her lips together to blend the color, then turned toward me and struck a playful pose. "What do you think?"

"You look amazing," I admitted.

It was true. I often forgot that Mom was beautiful. I wondered if I'd ever be beautiful too, after all my *late blooming* was behind me.

Mom stepped into a pair of low-heeled pumps. Then she walked out of the bathroom into the hallway, dipping a finger in the little porcelain holy water font on the wall and flicking some drops of wetness onto herself and me.

I winced. "Hey. I thought you don't believe in all Grandma's God stuff."

"Well, I guess it can't hurt." Mom threw her purse over her shoulder. "We need all the luck we can get."

She twisted the deadbolts, slid the chain locks open, and walked out the door.

"Re-lock behind me," she said. I nodded, and stood by the door a moment, listening to her pumps click-clacking all the way down three flights of stairs.

In the bathroom, I pulled on a pair of jean shorts and my favorite T-shirt. It said, "This is How I Roll," beneath a smiling cartoon sushi character. Then I brushed my hair back into a ponytail and checked myself out in the mirror. My face was pale and freckled, and my straight brown hair hung limply. Just an ugly duckling hoping to turn into a swan someday.

The cinnamon smell was stronger than ever, wafting from the kitchen. I walked in there and saw Grandma dressed for work, slathering butter onto a piece of raisin toast. She looked up approvingly at me.

"At least one of you is an early bird," she said. "A go-getter, like me, huh?"

I shrugged. She gestured for me to sit down at the table.

"Come have some toast and tea," she said.

I didn't disobey.

"Mom was up early too," I told her. "She went looking for a job."

Grandma sighed. "I wish her the best," she said. "But your mother should have finished the court stenographer school that I paid for years ago. Then she'd have a good career. Something she could always fall back on."

I crunched into the slice of toast Grandma placed in front of me. Buttery, cinnamon-y goodness.

"What's a court stenographer?" I asked in between bites.

"Someone who sits in a courtroom and types up everything everyone says during a trial, using a special machine," she explained. "It's the person who creates the official record that the judge looks at to decide the case."

"It sounds important," I said. I couldn't picture Mom wanting to do anything like that.

"It is!" Grandma replied. "Very important indeed! But my rebellious daughter didn't follow through, of course.

Instead, she ran off with that …" Her voice trailed off. She patted my hand brusquely. "Anyway. No use dwelling in the past."

I appreciated that she refrained from tearing into my dad right in front of me. Obviously, that's where she was going. I finished my toast, sipped my tea, and looked at the clock on the wall. It was the old-fashioned kind, with a picture of a rooster on it for some reason, and two hands and the numbers around the circle. I always forgot how to read these kinds of clocks. I'd learned how in first grade. But I promptly forgot, because why bother when you can just look at a phone to see what time it is, and you don't have to remember which hand is which.

"I'll be at St. Brendan's all day," Grandma said. "Someone has to bring home a paycheck around here. So, since your mother ran off without saying *boo*, looks like you kids will be here on your own for a while. You'll manage all right?"

"Yeah, we'll be fine," I responded. We were used to being alone.

"You're the eldest," Grandma said. "Judith and Dylan are under your watch. It's an important responsibility."

"Ha!" I replied. "Judith doesn't listen to me. She does what she wants. If I had to guess, she'll probably watch makeup tutorials online all day."

"Hmmph. That won't do at all," Grandma said. "I'll have to bring her down to the Boys and Girls Club when I get home. I'll sign her up for day camp so she doesn't loaf around rotting her brain all summer."

She reached over to the kitchen drawer, pulled out a pad and pen, and started scribbling.

"I don't think Judith will want to go to camp," I warned her.

"And I don't recall asking what Judith will want," said Grandma curtly.

She tore the top piece of paper off the pad and handed it to me with a flourish.

"What's this?" I asked, taking the paper and trying to make out her swirly cursive writing.

"Chore lists for the three of you," she said matter-of-factly.

I protested. "But ... we're on summer break.

"There's work to be done around here," Grandma insisted, "and I have four able-bodied people living here with me now. Read it and let me know if you have any questions."

Here's what she had written down:

Judith
Sweep Floors
Clean kitchen / Do dishes
Tidy bathroom / Hang fresh towels

Dylan
Take trash to chute
Tidy living room / Fluff sofa pillows
Dust saint statues (carefully!)

Vicki
Get groceries
Make breakfast and lunch for Judith and Dylan
Tidy bedroom / Make beds

"How am I supposed to know what to get at the grocery store?" I asked.

Grandma slapped a twenty-dollar bill and a shopping list down on the tabletop, and gulped down the remaining tea in her cup. From a drawer, she pulled out a keychain in the shape of a dove. She held it up in front of my face.

"The square key is for the front door downstairs, and the other three are for the deadbolts," she instructed. "You're smart, so you'll figure out which one is which. Met Food is just a short walk. You'll be able to ask your phone to help you get there, no doubt. Those blasted gadgets know everything now, don't they?"

I nodded, following Grandma down the hall to the front door.

"Red apples," Grandma specified as she walked. "Green are too sour. And make sure there are no bruises on the fruit. Dom at the butcher counter knows the cut of meat I like, so introduce yourself, and tell him it's for me." She buttoned up her sweater and dipped her fingers in the holy water, doing the sign of the cross on her forehead and chest.

I stared at the list and the twenty dollars in my hand. I couldn't believe Grandma would trust me to do the shopping. And she had called me *smart*.

"Okay," I said, nodding. "I got this."

"And bring back my change," Grandma added sternly. With that, she turned on her heel and left the apartment. I instinctively calculated how much I would have in my Amtrak fund if I were to just add this twenty to what was already in my ladybug wallet. I stood there considering for a moment what would happen if I just took off for California right then and there.

But I wasn't a thief. Anyway, I was supposed to meet Rosa in an hour. I had to feed Dylan. And try to get Judith out of bed. And buy the right kind of red apples at Met Food. I couldn't possibly leave now. Soon enough, I told myself.

When Dylan woke up, I fed him a bowl of Cheerios with sliced banana and a glass of orange juice.

"Breakfast is served, sir!" I announced, handing him a spoon, and feeling rather proud of myself for accomplishing one of the things on my chore list without Grandma telling me how wrong I was doing it.

"How come you're acting like you're a grown-up?" Dylan asked suspiciously. "You're just a kid."

"I'm your big sister, and I just gave you breakfast. How about saying thank you?"

Dylan thought about that for a second.

"All right. Thank you." He shoveled a spoonful of Cheerios into his mouth.

Judith wasn't as cooperative. No big surprise. She had to be dragged out of bed, and when I tried to get her to eat something, she said she wasn't hungry. She took one look at the chore list and laughed. "Yeah, right."

Then she went into the living room and curled up in Mom's blanket on the living room sofa. She clicked on the TV, staring blankly at a show where five ladies were sitting around a table with coffee cups yelling over each other about something. Maybe the Boys and Girls Club camp wouldn't be the worst thing for her. If anyone could make her do it, Grandma could.

I didn't have time to fight with my sister: it was almost ten o'clock. Time to go meet Rosa.

"I'm going out to get the groceries now. So please do the dishes while I'm gone," I pleaded.

"Sure. You can bet on it," muttered Judith, not looking away from the TV. As I walked away, I heard her add: "… NOT!"

I patted the twenty dollars and shopping list in my pocket, and clutching the dove keyring in my hand, unlocked the door, stepped over the threshold, and suddenly, ... *I was free.*

CHAPTER 7

I BOUNDED DOWN the stairs, picking up my pace on the third-floor landing, acutely aware of the moment I passed apartment 3D, where I imagined Miss Kirby crouched behind the door lying in wait, ready to spring out and grab me in an instant. I kept reciting imaginary license plate numbers over and over in my head and didn't breathe until I had dashed past her door and scrambled down to the safety of the second floor. Smells of spices and soaps wafted through cracks beneath closed apartment doors. A hodgepodge of muffled sounds filled the stairwell: the sprinkle of a shower, the squeal of a tea kettle, a radio announcer's voice speaking in a language I couldn't identify. A newscaster saying the subway flasher had struck again, and was still evading police.

On the ground floor, the building's entrance boasted two rows of metal mailboxes that lined the wall like antique miniature doorways leading into tenants' lives. Each one had a neatly affixed handwritten label: Vega, Nikolaev, De La Santo, Morales, Fuentes, Henries, Agani-Pierce, Magbanua, Hassan, Kirby, Purvis, Casey, Paperny, Dafallah … So many names. Who were they all? What were they doing? How did they end up here, of all places? I got a jolt of excitement thinking about it—like the whole entire world could somehow be made to fit right there in that one building.

I swung open the front door, and there, on the top step of the stoop, a girl sat with her back to me. She had long, black, shiny hair in two neat braids. She spun around.

In the broad daylight I took in Rosa's big, chestnut brown eyes; long eyelashes; full mouth; straight, broad nose; and thick, arched black eyebrows. She wore small gold hoops in her ears, blue jeans, and a pink hoodie with a faded picture of a palm tree on it. Just like the palm trees in all my daydreams about California. *It must be a sign.*

She smiled, revealing two crooked front teeth that barely overlapped one another. This tiny imperfection only made her look even more exquisite. She held up the little plastic figurine.

"Here, have your Blessed Mother back."

She tossed it. I managed to catch it and tucked it safely in my pocket.

"Ha. Thanks."

"I heard you just moved here from the boonies?" asked Rosa.

"What's that?"

"Like the countryside. The middle of nowhere?"

"You're not wrong. I'm from upstate."

"Well, I can show you around the neighborhood if you want, so you know what's up," Rosa said.

"That'd be great!" I answered.

A man dressed all in leather with a big round helmet came out the front door and squeezed past us on his way down the steps, grunting what I guessed was meant to be a greeting or an 'excuse me.' He got onto a black motorcycle parked in front of the building, revved loudly, then peeled away.

"That's Vlad," said Rosa. "Apartment 3A. He can somehow afford a fancy motorcycle, but I heard my pops saying he's always late on his rent."

A brigade of young moms marched up the sidewalk at a quick pace, pushing baby strollers and talking together in Spanish. They all called *'buenos dias'* to Rosa as they passed by.

Rosa waved.

"You know everyone around here?" I asked.

"Pretty much," she said proudly. "Pops is like the unofficial mayor of the neighborhood, because he takes care of the block. Chased some troublemakers away when he first took over as super of the building. Cleaned the graffiti. So now everyone loves him."

That must be nice, I thought, *having a dad like that.*

"Who else is in your family?" I asked.

"I'm an only child," Rosa explained. "It's just me, Papi, and Mami. Mami's studying to be a nurse. What about you?"

"I have a younger brother and sister," I said.

"Luckyyyy!" exclaimed Rosa.

"Not really," I said. "They can be super annoying."

"What about your parents?" Rosa asked.

I spoke without thinking, and the words that spilled out of my mouth were a surprise even to me.

"Well," I said, "my mom is a court stenographer. And my dad lives in California."

Then, as if that wasn't impressive enough, I added: "He's kinda famous."

In an instant, Rosa's expression changed. She looked intrigued … maybe even a bit jealous?

"Is he a movie star or something?" she asked.

I nodded while my mind raced to identify someone. "You know the guy who plays Iron Man?" I said nonchalantly. "That's my dad."

Rosa's eyes tripled in size. "Are you messing with me?" she yelped. "I want to be a famous actress and singer when I grow up! In a couple weeks, I'm going to a summer performing arts institute in Manhattan. I had to audition to get in and everything."

"That's cool," I said, trying to steady my voice from shaking.

Rosa clasped her hands together like she was praying. "Do you think maybe your dad can get me a part in one of his movies someday?"

My heart raced with the adrenaline of telling such big, fat lies to my new friend.

"It's possible," I said. "I'll ask him. I'm going to visit him pretty soon."

Which wasn't actually a lie; it's just that he didn't know it yet.

"OMG, thank you!" Rosa shouted, throwing her arms around me.

I squirmed, suddenly very nervous about having to continue this lie I had started.

"I have to go to Met Food for my grandma," I said, changing the subject.

"I'll walk you there," offered Rosa.

"You don't have to," I shrugged. "I can just ask Siri how to get there."

Rosa swatted me playfully.

"Forget Siri. My parents won't let me have a phone. I was the only kid in eighth grade without one, which really sucked. But they said maybe next year in high school I can get one."

She stood up and bounded down the stoop steps. "C'mon. Let's go the long way so I can show you around the neighborhood."

I made sure to steer the subject away from my father after that by asking Rosa questions about anything and everything we passed. She walked like royalty, the daughter of the unofficial mayor of Bainbridge Avenue, strolling through her kingdom describing important landmarks like the laundromat, the corner bodega, Nino's Pizzeria where they had fifteen flavors of Italian ice, and the barking Doberman locked behind a chain link fence.

She warned me to avoid the yellow house with the gnomes out front. You have to hold your breath when you walk past, she said, because the people who live there are always smoking pot and you might get high if you breathe in the skunky air.

We walked past a daycare center, a *pupuseria*, a *muy thai* martial arts studio, and a hair salon advertising African braids. One right turn and a block later, we were at the park. It in no way resembled the expansive leafy greenness of parks in upstate New York. This one was tiny in comparison, and didn't have much nature in it at all. Just a few meager trees, benches on a concrete path, a sparse patch of grass, a crumbling bandstand, and a playground with equipment that appeared to be as old as Grandma. On the far side of the park was an odd black building that looked aerodynamic, like an enormous black bird that might take off in flight at any moment, and behind that a small white wooden cottage, extremely out of place and dwarfed by the tall apartment buildings surrounding the little park on all sides.

Rosa tapped on a plaque at the park's entrance and said, "Back in the day a famous poet used to live in that house over there."

I stopped and looked at the words on the plaque. They said:

> *Built in 1812, the cottage was the last home of Edgar Allan Poe, one of America's greatest writers.*

"Believe it or not, the Bronx used to be the boonies back then, like where you're from," Rosa explained. "So, this house used to be surrounded by fields and trees."

She closed her eyes and inhaled deeply, as if transporting herself back in time.

I closed my eyes too, but my creative visualization exercise was interrupted by a swarm of teenage boys zooming past on skateboards. They were loud and boisterous, calling out to one another, scraping their wheels along the curb, flipping and slapping the boards on the ground, attempting to jump up and land on benches and metal railings that separated the walkways from the grass. One of the boys wiped out violently, landing on the pavement. His board came skidding over toward us. Miraculously, I was able to stop it with my foot before it crashed directly into my shin at high speed. The boy popped up like nothing had happened.

"James!" shouted Rosa. "You almost knocked my friend over. Watch yourself!"

In spite of itself, my heart did a little flip when Rosa referred to me as her *friend*.

"Sorry," the boy shouted, jogging over to retrieve his board.

He looked about my age and height with a stocky build and overgrown straight black bangs that fell below his eyebrows. His eyes were dark brown. He wore a red T-shirt, black basketball shorts, and ragged checkerboard Vans. He brushed his hair out of his face and looked at me, which made the tiny hairs on the back of my neck tingle. I definitely wasn't used to being looked at by boys.

"Sushi girl, huh?" he remarked, with a crooked grin.

I was caught off guard. "What?"

He pointed to my shirt. "This is how you roll?"

I let out a nervous laugh. "Oh, yeah. I guess." I hoped I didn't sound dumb.

James winked. "Ok, that's lit, sushi girl. Seeya!" He hopped back on his board and scooted away, calling to his friends, "Yo! Did you see that wipeout?"

Rosa put her arm around my shoulder. "He lives in our building. 2B. You have to watch out for him though. He's trouble." She paused a second. "And he was definitely checking you out."

I could feel my face getting red. "Seriously? I thought he was making fun of me."

"Most of the time with these boys, it's hard to tell the difference," Rosa said knowingly. "They don't know how to act. Extremely immature."

"Boys are basically the same way up in the boonies," I sighed. "Confusing."

Rosa laughed. "You're weird," she said. "And I like weird." She put her arm around my shoulder and squeezed me close to her. I guess my body must've stiffened, because she said, "Sorry, I'm just a very physically affectionate person. Does it bother you?"

"No," I said. Which was only half true. We weren't huggy in my family, and I had limited experience with friends. Her squeeze made me feel a little uncomfortable, but I didn't hate it, exactly.

"I hope you don't go off to California right away," Rosa said. "There's no one my age in the building to chill with, except James. And my Papi doesn't want me hanging out with him."

"Why?" I asked.

"Like I said," Rosa answered, "he's chasing trouble. He's bad in school, got suspended for vaping, hangs around the skaters all over the city. He's a bad-boy type, you know?"

I nodded. "I probably won't go to Cali *right away*," I assured her. "Plans are up in the air at the moment."

That's something I'd heard Mom say. "Up in the air" means "may never happen."

But this time, *this* plan—me going to California—*was* going to happen. I had invested too much of my heart and mind into planning it, and I would make sure it happened, no matter what.

CHAPTER 8

I MANAGED TO reinstall the Virgin Mary—only a bit worse for the wear with a small nick in her blue plastic veil—back on the windowsill without Grandma noticing she was gone.

And in fact, Grandma was so pleased with my first shopping expedition that, after that, she made Met Food one of my regular chores, and even let me keep a dollar from the change each time. A few days went by, and my ladybug wallet was getting fatter and fatter, reaching an account balance of $111—the luckiest of sums. I was feeling optimistic about my upcoming journey.

And maybe, just maybe, the holy water thing was working after all, because Mom landed a temporary administrative assistant job at a construction company.

"It's just for three months, while the real assistant is on maternity leave," said Mom, with excitement. "But it'll give me time to look for something permanent." At dinner the night she made the announcement, she demonstrated how she'd be answering the phones:

"Perna Construction, how may I help you?" she said in a cheerful voice.

The pay was $22 an hour, which was four dollars an hour more than Mom had earned at the last job she'd had upstate.

Dylan gleefully tossed Mr. Choofie in the air and caught him. "Yay! We're finally rich!"

"We're not rich, Dyl," scoffed Judith. "Not even close. Calm down."

"*And* … I have even more good news," Mom told us. "I have a date tonight! With a policeman."

Mom's picker being what it was, this was decidedly *not* good news in my opinion.

"A policeman?" asked Dylan, eyes widening. "Does he have a motorcycle?"

"No." Mom tousled Dylan's hair and let out a giddy laugh that grated on my nerves. "He drives a squad car."

"With a siren?" asked Dylan.

"Yup."

"Is he one of those corrupt cops like on the news?" asked Judith bluntly.

"Stop watching *Live at Five*, Judith," snapped Mom.

"Excuse *me* for wanting to be informed," Judith protested.

Mom brushed her off. "I've got to get ready. Vinnie will be picking me up soon."

"Vinnie? Not *Vinnie Delgado*?" asked Grandma.

"The one and only." Mom grinned. She floated down the hallway toward the bathroom. Judith kicked Dylan's shin under the table to formally register her disapproval of Mom having a date.

"Ow!" howled Dylan, pounding on the table.

A floor below, Miss Kirby immediately started banging with her broom handle. That old crow was always down there poised and ready, just waiting to hear the teensiest noise.

"Shhh!" Judith teased Dylan. "Or the witch will come for you."

"Who's this Vinnie Delgado?" I asked Grandma.

"He went to high school with your mother."

"Were they boyfriend–girlfriend?"

"It was something like that," remembered Grandma. "Vincent was a nice boy. His family was in church every Sunday. Good people."

"Being in church doesn't make them good people, Grandma," Judith pointed out. "Some priests are real pervs, you know. I watched a whole documentary about it."

Grandma frowned. "Sadly, I can't say that's incorrect. But you should really stay off that YouTube. You're filling your head with all these vile things."

"That's the point," quipped Judith. "Knowledge is power."

Grandma, not knowing how to respond, turned away from Judith to address me and Dylan with her next remark.

"As I was saying," she continued, "Vincent is from a nice family. I heard that he owns a detached house in Pelham Bay. Wonderful neighborhood. Tree-lined block. Word is, he bought it for a good price and fixed it up himself."

Twenty minutes later, Mom breezed out of the bathroom, the scent of hairspray and lotion wafting behind her. She swatted me playfully on the butt as she passed.

"Mom, *stop*." I disliked it when Mom got in one of her happy, silly moods. It was almost as annoying as when she was indifferent.

When the buzzer rang later, Mom ran down the hallway to the intercom and pressed the button.

"Hello?" she said into the little box on the wall.

A man's garbled voice came through the speaker: "It's Vinnie." Mom pressed the button to buzz him in to unlock the front door downstairs.

She opened the door to our apartment, and we all gathered behind her, listening to the sounds of Officer Delgado's heavy footsteps making their way up the stairs.

When he finally came huffing into view, it was frankly a bit of a disappointment. First off, he wasn't wearing a policeman's uniform, just a regular old sweater and black jeans. He was shorter than Mom, and balding slightly. An average potato-shaped head. He held a bouquet of flowers and extended them for Mom.

"Ooh, thank you, Vinnie!" Mom gushed.

Gag. She had acted this way with every guy she dated since my dad left us. They were each supposed to be our ticket out of a crappy life, but none of them stuck around long. Then after they bailed, Mom was guaranteed to be in bad spirits for months. I eyed Officer Delgado skeptically. He made his way through the door and pecked Grandma on the cheek.

"Hey there, Mrs. Casey. Long time, no see."

Grandma held him at arm's length. "Look at you, all grown up! A police officer like your dad."

Officer Delgado nodded. "Yes, ma'am. Been on the force nearly fifteen years now."

"I was so sorry to hear of your mother's passing, of course."

"Thank you."

Mom shoved the flowers toward Grandma. "Could you put these in water please, Ma?" Then she gestured to me, Judith, and Dylan. "Well! Say hello. Where are your manners?"

That was rich. Mom pretending we'd been well trained.

"Hello," I said dryly.

"Where's your badge?" asked Dylan.

"Are you carrying?" asked Judith.

Officer Delgado showed them his badge and his holster. That shut them both up for the time being.

Grandma took Judith and me into the kitchen and taught us how to prepare tea the proper way, and how to put biscuits on a plate so they looked attractive and could be served to guests. She even let us bring the tray out and serve tea to Mom and Officer Delgado in the living room. As they sipped their tea, Dylan acted out a cops and robbers scene to show off in front of Officer Delgado. In this scenario, Dylan was the cop, and Mr. Choofie was the robber. Dylan took Choofie down, cuffed him, and sent him to jail under the coffee table. Officer Delgado laughed and clapped.

"We need good guys like you on the force," he said. Dylan beamed.

Then Mom stood up. "See, I told you they were a trip," she said to Officer Delgado. Then she turned to us. "We have to go now, my darlings," she cooed. "Be good for Grandma, and don't stay up too late."

She never, ever called us her "darlings," so obviously she was trying to show off in front of Officer Delgado.

For dinner that night, Grandma heated up fish sticks in the oven. The small kitchen was stuffy from the oven being on. We opened up all the windows in the apartment. A light summer breeze rustled the lace curtain in the kitchen. It felt good. Judith was nervously talking the whole time because she was starting basketball camp at the Boys and Girls Club the next day. She always talked nonstop when she was nervous.

"I'll probably make friends, but if not, I don't care," Judith said.

"Of course you will, don't be foolish!" This was Grandma's way of reassuring her.

As we were clearing the table after eating, we heard a musical tune from outside the open window. That meant one thing: the ice cream truck was coming up the block.

"Serial killer vibes," commented Judith.

"Ooooh! Can we get ice cream?" squealed Dylan. "Pretty please?"

Grandma went into her bag, but she didn't have enough cash. I looked at Dylan's eager face and made a snap decision to bust into my ladybug wallet. Just this once. A few bucks wouldn't make or break my California fund, and anyway, I was seriously in the mood for a strawberry shortcake bar.

We ran downstairs, worried that the ice cream truck would pull away before we made it to the street. Miss

Kirby's door opened a crack as we passed by the third-floor landing, and all we could see was darkness inside her apartment, but she hissed at us, which made us fly even faster.

On Bainbridge Avenue, all the kids from the block were outside, crowding around the truck as it chimed merrily. The sun was going down behind the buildings across the street, giving Bainbridge Avenue a warm orange glow. When it was my turn at the truck's window, I ordered myself a strawberry shortcake, plus a SpongeBob popsicle for Dylan and a rocket pop for Judith.

We sat on the stoop eating our treats with a feeling of simple satisfaction. Rosa, in her living room, stuck her head out her first story window.

"Come out and get ice cream," I offered. "I have money."

"I can't," Rosa said. "Mami's making dinner. I'm not allowed to ruin my appetite." She looked at Judith and Dylan. "Is this your bro and sis?"

I nodded. "Dylan, Judith, meet my friend Rosa."

They could barely break themselves away from their desserts to look up and acknowledge her. Judith managed a "Yo." I pinched her in the arm for being rude.

"Sorry," I said to Rosa. "You'd think they'd never had dessert before. Or interacted with other humans."

Rosa laughed. "I always wanted a brother and sister. Being an only child is completely boring."

"Oh really? I'll trade you," I said. "Why don't you come up and sleep in the same room with these two spazzes tonight?"

"Hey!" objected Dylan, frowning and looking up from his melting SpongeBob. "You can't trade us! You're our big sister. Family's forever no matter how crazy they make you."

"Says who?" I asked.

"Grandma told me that, so it must be true," answered Dylan. He had sticky yellow sherbet all over his chin and the front of his T-shirt.

"Tell that to Dad," scoffed Judith. I pinched her again so she'd shut up. I didn't want my lies to Rosa to be exposed by my stupid sister.

"Oh, well," I said to Rosa. "Looks like I'm stuck with them."

Dylan rested his head contentedly on my shoulder.

CHAPTER 9

THE DAYS AND weeks went by. Rosa and I met on the stoop every day, and whispered together in the airshaft every night after Judith and Dylan fell asleep. Some days, when the temperatures outside got up into the nineties, Rosa and I went to the Poe Park Visitor Center or the public library, to soak up their air conditioning. I learned that the poet guy named Poe had written a long poem all about a freaky raven who he thought was talking to him, which hit just a bit too close to home. Grandma called those days "scorchers," and Bainbridge Avenue came alive in a chaotic, fun way, with the ice cream truck making frequent rounds up the block, blaring its warped, tinkling tune. Neighbors set out folding chairs on the sidewalk and sat talking and laughing until the streetlights came on, their feet soaking in wading pools filled with cool water, while kids ran and played in the spray let loose from garden hoses and fire hydrants.

Being with Rosa was easy, and it felt good to have a friend. We never seemed to get bored of each other. We talked about all kinds of things: movies and music, and who we thought we would marry someday, and how nervous we were to start high school in the fall. Sometimes I felt overwhelmed by an urge to tell Rosa the truth about my mom and dad, but I always stopped myself. From everything she shared with me about her parents, it seemed like they were the perfect family. I didn't want her to judge us harshly, or think I was deranged for lying in the first place. I also didn't want her to try to talk me out of going to California, so I kept my mouth shut, even though I felt like a fraud whenever she brought up my dad the famous actor or my mom the court stenographer.

The day before Rosa's performing arts institute was about to start, she said she wanted to show me something special. Mom was at work, Judith was at camp, and Dylan was with Grandma at St. Brendan's. So, after I finished my morning chores, I met Rosa down on the stoop, like usual.

"Follow me," she whispered, a glimmer in her eye.

She led me around to the side of the apartment building. Behind a flimsy layer of chicken wire, a narrow passageway was revealed, separating our building from the one next door. Rosa pulled the chicken wire aside and ducked into the passageway.

"Where are we going?" I asked.

"Don't worry. It's nothing scary, supernatural, or punishable by law," Rosa assured me.

I ducked in behind her. "Okay," I said. "I trust you."

"Well, technically, maybe it *is* punishable by some crazy law," she corrected herself. "But I seriously doubt they'd enforce it."

My throat felt dry. To relax, I tried to recall some license plates. But my memory was foggy. Since Rosa and I had been spending so much time together, I hadn't been doing my license plate thing as much as before. I had someone to talk to now, someone to distract me from my daydreams and the mind tricks I was accustomed to playing with myself.

I trudged along behind Rosa. Random trash littered our path. We walked between the two buildings, dead grass crunching beneath our feet. Rosa navigated past an old plastic kiddie wading pool propped on its side. A busted wheelchair. Empty beer cans. A pizza box. A plastic Met Food bag full of shoes.

At the rear of the building there was a green door. Rosa reached into her sweatshirt and produced a key on a ball chain that hung around her neck.

"Another perk to being the super's daughter," she grinned. "Master key."

I gave her two thumbs up, nodding as if I understood what that meant.

What have I gotten myself into?

After unlocking the door, Rosa gave it a good, hard pull. She beckoned to me and looked around to make sure no one was watching as we slipped inside. When she closed the door behind us, it was pitch dark. I pulled my phone from my back pocket and tried in vain to turn on the flashlight function. Nervous, fumbling, I held my breath to avoid inhaling the musty odor.

Rosa hit a wall switch. Bare light bulbs in fixtures on the ceiling flickered on. She took my hand and led me down a concrete staircase into the building's basement.

Rows of metal cages lined the walls. Inside them was a menagerie of pure creepiness: rusted bicycles, boxes stacked upon boxes, old chairs, a typewriter from the olden days, once-used camping equipment. All of it covered with a layer of dust.

"I thought you said this *wasn't* going to be scary," I hissed.

"I lied a teensy bit," Rosa chuckled. "But don't worry, it's safe. You're fine."

We walked past the cages. I tried to avoid looking directly at a horrifying rocking horse with one eye, noting it out of my peripheral vision and feeling certain it would appear in my nightmares later.

"What is all this stuff?" I asked.

"There's a storage locker for each apartment in the building," Rosa explained.

"These don't look like any lockers I've ever seen before," I said. They looked more like cages that would be used to trap enormous animals, like hippopotamuses.

"That's just what we call them," said Rosa. "They're basically full of people's junk. Hardly anyone ever comes down here. They get my dad to store stuff away and then usually forget all about it."

In the last cage on the end, my mom's magenta suitcase caught my eye from where it lay on the dusty floor.

Rosa turned to face me, staring deep into my eyes with intensity.

"Pinky promise you won't tell anyone what I'm about to show you," she said.

She held her pinky out. All business.

"Okay, fine," I said, curling my pinky tightly around Rosa's.

"That's a binding vow," said Rosa. She took my hand again, walking me around a corner and even deeper into a cavernous space with a little alcove and another door. She opened that door, and a triangle of gray light streamed in through a dusty window near the ceiling.

I heard meowing. As my eyes adjusted to the dim light, I saw cat eyes shining brightly. I couldn't be sure how many eyes there were. Definitely more than two.

"Welcome to my underground lair ... *Mwah, ha, ha!*" announced Rosa. She opened a bin and took out a bag of cat food, filling two bowls sitting on the floor. Two little cats immediately came over to eat. One was cream colored, and the other had orange and brown stripes.

"Meet Angelica Schuyler and Mr. Thing," Rosa said, pointing to each of them in turn.

I scanned the space. I could now see that it had been furnished into a makeshift living room. An old-fashioned bench-style car seat, olive green and held intact with duct tape, sat on a carpet scrap. Milk crates served as end tables. A kitty play structure had been made out of cardboard boxes. A litter pan was on the ground near the window, and it didn't even stink too bad. It was obvious someone had been taking special care of the space. And that someone was clearly Rosa.

"What *is* this place?" I asked in wonderment.

"A secret hideout. My little escape from the world. Sweet, isn't it?"

"Very. You did this all by yourself?"

"Yup!" Rosa plopped down on the car seat/sofa proudly. She retrieved a cat comb from the milk crate and began brushing the cream-colored cat's fur with it.

"Angelica loves to be combed," she said. The cat made a gentle purring sound.

The orange-striped one, Mr. Thing, rubbed against my leg, and I reached down to pet its softness.

"Papi would ground me for life if he found out I was down here," Rosa continued. "Plus, there's no pets allowed in the building. Landlord's dumb rules. We could get in big trouble, so you can't tell a soul about this."

I crossed my heart with my hand. "Your secret is safe with me."

Rosa told me about how on her last day of eighth grade a month earlier, she was walking home from school and she heard mewing coming from behind an abandoned fruit stand. Two tiny kittens. She waited and waited but their mama did not return. So, Rosa wrapped them in a sweatshirt, snuck them home, and nursed them back to health down in the back room of the basement. She was looking for permanent homes for them. In the meantime, she had them set up like a king and queen in her secret hideaway.

We sat in silence petting the cats.

"What do you need to escape from?" I asked Rosa.

"What do you mean?" she said.

"You said it's your escape, down here," I reminded her.

"Oh, I don't know," she replied. "I guess from my parents, school stress, that kind of thing. The usual."

"Your folks sound like they're pretty great, though," I ventured, letting Mr. Thing hop into my lap. He was getting comfortable with me. I scratched underneath his chin.

"Oh, my folks *are* great," Rosa said. "Totally. And I love them like crazy. It's just …" She shrugged. "They can be strict. Like the no cell phone thing."

I nodded.

"And then there's all the *hopes* and *dreams* they have for me," she added. That line she delivered dramatically, sarcastically.

"How dare they!" I joked.

"Sure. No, They're awesome. But it can feel like a lot of pressure sometimes."

I nodded again to show that I understood and was there for her. But of course, I didn't. And I wasn't. I would be on my way to California before too long. My mom didn't have any hopes or dreams for me that I was aware of. She could barely take care of herself. Maybe my dad had once had hopes or dreams for me. No way of knowing for sure, but I liked to think he did.

Petting Mr. Thing methodically, I wondered how often my father even thought of me. I tried to picture what he would look like after all the time that had passed—the surprised expression that would come over his face when he opened his front door and saw his eldest daughter standing there on the front porch, not a little girl anymore, having made her way across the country all by herself. To find him. And maybe, to make things right again.

"Hello? Earth to Vicki," Rosa was saying. I snapped back to the present moment.

"You were like a million miles away there."

Two thousand eight hundred fifty miles, to be exact.

Rosa explained to me that since for the next two weeks she would be spending all day down at her performing arts institute in Manhattan, she needed me to take care of the cats. Feed them, clean their litter boxes, brush them, and play with them daily. I was the only one she could trust.

"Of course, you can count on me," I told her. The truth was, I was glad to add caring for the cats to my daily chore list. At least they'd keep me company. It would be pretty lonely during the day without my friend around. And I had another, more selfish reason to accept the job. With Ernesto's master key, I could see once and for all what my mother was hiding in that magenta suitcase of hers. Something told me I might find a clue as to my father's whereabouts and what really happened that drove him away from us.

CHAPTER 10

THAT NIGHT, ROSA invited me to have dinner with her family. Walking into apartment 1A for the first time, I immediately recognized the layout of Rosa's home as the mirror opposite of Grandma's apartment upstairs. But the walls in the Rodriguez family's long narrow hallway were filled with framed photos and colorful paintings, contrasting with Grandma's lonesome holy water font and beige plaster. A pungent cooking smell hung in the air.

In the living room, there was a large, ornate oval frame boasting Rosa's parents' formal wedding portrait. I could see that Rosa looked a lot like her mother, who was dressed like a princess in the photo, with dramatic eye makeup and with curls in her black hair creating cascading waves. Young Ernesto looked handsome and happy, with chiseled cheekbones, dark hair, and no mustache. They were posed in a beautiful garden with colorful blossoms all around them.

Surrounding the wedding photograph was an array of smaller framed photos. Rosa saw me looking and began to describe her extended family members who were pictured.

"Those are my grandparents, in Ecuador," she said. She went on to point to other smiling faces in frames: aunts, uncles, and cousins.

Upstairs at Grandma's, there were no framed photos. Only my well-hidden family snapshot from the apple orchard. And there was one other secret photo, one I was sure I wasn't even supposed to know about. A photo of my grandfather, Tom Casey, in his military uniform when he was a young man in something called Operation Desert Storm. Tom was my mom's father. I happened to know there was a photo of him tucked in the corner of the mirror above Grandma's dresser, in her bedroom. I had seen it that one time years before, when I had snuck into Grandma's room while she and Mom were in the kitchen embroiled in the infamous Dylan Baptism Brawl of 2015. The day I hid in the mahogany wardrobe. Naturally, seeing the photo had made me curious. After all, no one had ever even mentioned my grandfather in my presence. But on the drive home, Mom was mad. So when I'd innocently asked her about him, she told me to pipe down and be good. She said that he died when she was young and it wasn't a happy story, and she didn't want to talk about him. Ever. So that was the end of that.

I smiled politely as Rosa described the people in the photographs, but I felt jealous looking at her big, close-knit family. Every known member of my family was right upstairs in apartment 4D. With the exception of my dad, of course. Mom was an only child. Dad didn't have any family, as far as I knew. Seemed like Rosa could spare a few extended family members for me. There were scores of proud Rodriguezes beaming down at me from their polished frames.

When I turned around, I saw that the opposite wall in their living room was a straight-up Rosa shrine. A bazillion portraits of her over the years. *Preschool graduation Rosa* in a canary yellow cap and gown. *First Communion Rosa* with a white veil and gloves. *Sporty pigtail Rosa* holding a soccer ball. And a dozen awards boasting her name: Model Citizen, Super Reader, Science Fair Winner, Sportsmanship, Math Master.

"Jeez. Is there anything you're *not* good at?" I joked. "Where's your Nobel Prize?"

Rosa rolled her eyes and made a "stop it" gesture with her hand, like it was no big deal. "My parents are over-the-top. They live for this stuff. To be honest, I wish they'd chill sometimes."

She led me down her hallway, stopping in the kitchen to grab two chocolate chip granola bars from the cupboard. Then she opened her bedroom door. Like the room upstairs that I was sharing with Judith and Dylan, the sole window in Rosa's room looked out onto the airshaft. But that's where the similarities between the two rooms ended. Rosa's window was decorated with cheerful pink polka dot curtains. Her floors were polished smooth, accented with a little fluffy rug. All the furniture matched. Neat pine dresser, bookshelf, desk, bed board, and vanity—a perfect set. The lavender comforter and pillows looked comfy and soft.

I scoured my mind to come up with a license plate number to focus on so I wouldn't burst from envy. Why was I the one whose dad didn't care a rat's behind about her? What made Rosa so much luckier, so much more lovable than me?

Mrs. Rodriguez finished making dinner, and Rosa and I set the table. The food was fried potato pancakes. Ernesto said it was a special dish from Ecuador. He thanked his wife for the food.

"Thank you, Mrs. Rodriguez," I said politely.

Rosa's mother smiled at me.

"You're welcome, sweetheart," she said. "Please, you can call me Arcelia."

Arcelia was the most beautiful name I had ever heard.

Before we ate, we all bowed our heads for a prayer, just like Grandma had taught us. Ernesto said a prayer in Spanish. Then he raised his glass and shouted, "*Salud!*"

Rosa raised hers too, echoing him: "*Salud!*"

I joined in, too, just a couple seconds behind. I hoped I was saying it right.

The food tasted yummy. For a second, seated around that cozy table, I imagined not going to California after all, but instead, living right down here with the Mayor of Bainbridge. Rosa and I would be like sisters, sharing that beautiful bedroom. Mom, Grandma, and Dylan would just be some noisy neighbors living upstairs on the fourth floor.

"Are you all ready for your big day tomorrow?" Arcelia asked Rosa between bites.

"Yes, Mami," Rosa answered.

Ernesto nodded, gesturing excitedly with his fork. "I know you'll be the best, *mi hija*. We are so proud of you."

"Our little star!" Arcelia said gleefully.

"Everyone's going to be really good there," Rosa explained. "I'm not even guaranteed to get cast in the production."

"Oh, you'll be cast," bellowed Ernesto, wagging his finger in the air. "Don't be ridiculous! You'll be the lead, *mi hija*."

Rosa smiled awkwardly and looked down at her plate.

After dinner, she slipped me her dad's master key, and I snuck it into the front pocket of my shorts. I thanked her parents for the lovely dinner, and ran two steps at a time up to the fourth floor. That key was burning like a flame in my pocket the whole rest of the evening. Like it somehow knew what I knew: that mysteries were about to be solved.

CHAPTER 11

THE NEXT MORNING when I woke up, the apartment was empty. Grandma brought Dylan to work with her in the parish office most days, and he liked it there. She even signed him up for the first Communion class, and Mom didn't protest this time. It seemed like she was too wrapped up in her romance with Officer Delgado—or "Uncle Vinnie," as we were now supposed to call him—to care much about her old anti-religious convictions anymore.

Vinnie picked Mom up from work almost every evening and brought her home late. Mom laughed a lot around him, and seemed to feel more relaxed than she had up in Middleton. Dylan and Judith were warming to Vinnie, too. He often brought Italian cookies over, and my little brother and sister were easy to impress. I still had my suspicions though. What would a nice, normal guy like him want with a woman who's broke and has three kids? Something had to be off. Life wasn't some fairy tale.

All alone in the apartment, the sound of the hen clock ticking was very loud, echoing off the walls. The master key felt like it weighed ten pounds in my pocket. I was nervous, but I knew it was time.

Once I got down to the basement though, I took one look at the magenta suitcase and chickened out. It took on a menacing glow, taunting me from behind the chain link of the storage cage. Maybe I was all talk. Because the truth was, when faced with the possibility of actually opening it and learning what was inside, I felt terrified about what I might find. What if my dad was dead? Or had another secret family that he loved better than us? Another daughter who he tucked into bed every night for the past five years? What if we had been replaced?

I went in to the cats, cleaned up after them, fed them, pet them, and brushed them. They kept looking around as if wondering where Rosa was.

When I was done caring for Mr. Thing and Angelica, I wandered out of the back room and looked down the eerie rows of storage cages. It fascinated me to see all the things that my neighbors kept there. What were people saving all this for?

"I have the key for two whole weeks," I said aloud, as if convincing myself. "I can take my time and work my way up to Mom's suitcase. I've waited this long, so there's no rush."

But while I was down there, I figured, what was the harm in using Ernesto's key to open some of the other apartments' lockers? Just to take an innocent little peek?

I opened up cage after cage. The tenants' storage lockers were a treasure trove. There were golf clubs, hockey sticks, gardening tools, old music collections on CDs and cassette tapes.

In locker #2C, James' "Citizen of the Month" certificate from first grade, along with a picture of little six-year-old him grinning, missing his two front teeth. There was a big laundry bag full of stuffed animals that looked well loved. Maybe James wasn't as tough as he tried to act. Would some awful guy really hang on to his childhood snuggly toys?

Marie Vega in 3B was a singer who'd had a record come out in the 1990s. There she was on the album cover with big hair, bright blue eye shadow, and a sequined off-the-shoulder top.

Mr. Henries in 1D saved an old wedding dress in a garment bag; a collection of vintage Troll dolls with fuzzy hair in every color of the rainbow; and boxes and boxes full of yellowing bills, birth certificates, tax returns, diplomas, and court summons'. Love letters, breakup letters, birthday cards, and condolence cards. And a picture of a lady on a fishing boat with the words *Carpe Diem* painted on the bow.

When Mr. Magbanua from 2A was a child, he was a baseball player. A pitcher who had made it to the Little League World Series. He threw a seventy-one-mile-per-hour curveball!

Miss Purvis from 4A had earned her certificate to teach American Sign Language. Mr. and Mrs. Morales, in 1C, had climbed mountains in Alaska, Washington State, and Peru. John Dafallah from 2C was on a game show in 1995 and came in second place and won $3,400. Vlad Paperny, the man with the motorcycle, had a folder full of love letters from an old sweetheart he had left behind in St. Petersburg, Russia. And Cheryl De Los Santos from 2D got an official commendation from the mayor for her work finding housing for people who had no place to go.

My chest thumped as I pored over these random things that surrounded me. I didn't have many belongings to call my own. Just the items hidden under my socks and underwear in the top drawer of the dresser, really. Seeing all those forgotten treasures in the basement storage units gave me an exhilarating, almost luxurious sensation. I knew there was special meaning ascribed to each yellowed file folder, rolled up poster, cracked teapot, and three-legged chair down there.

At the end of the row was locker #3D. Miss Kirby's. The cage's gate creaked open when I pushed it, and I heard one of the cats hiss from the back room. *This is precisely how people die in horror movies*, I thought. But apparently, I was willing to put myself in any kind of danger, as long as it didn't entail minding my own business or finding out the very things I had supposedly wanted so badly to know.

I was surprised that the first thing I saw in Miss Kirby's cage was a red bicycle with cobwebs on the handlebars and in the spokes. Plastic streamers dangled dejectedly out of the handlebar grips, having lost their sparkle long ago. I pulled the bike out and sat on it, moved the pedals. Its tires were flat, but other than that it seemed to be in almost perfect condition. *Wouldn't Dylan love a bicycle like that?* I mused.

I got off the bike and picked up an old, round cookie tin. My fingers trembled as I opened the rusty lid. Inside were newspaper clippings from sixty years ago about a fatal car accident. I read the article and saw the name Elise Kirby listed as the mother of the deceased. So, Miss Kirby hadn't always been a witchy old hermit. She had been someone's mom. And she lost her child. I felt my stomach turn and my eyes well up.

A strange chill came over me then, and I checked my phone to realize hours had gone by. I knew I had better get upstairs before my family came home and wondered where I was. As I locked up, I could hear the magenta suitcase in locker #4D teasing: "Victoria, what a loser you are. It's fine and good to nose your way into other people's lives and pasts, but you clearly don't have any guts when it comes to your own family secrets."

No one in the building was just who they appeared to be. They were all so much more than what I had seen of them going about their regular motions in the hallway, at the mailboxes, on the stoop. Everyone had secrets, not just us.

"Don't you worry, Miss Magenta Suitcase. I'll open you up next time," I said aloud again, gaining confidence. "I'm not afraid of you."

That, of course, was a lie.

I turned off the light and headed back upstairs.

CHAPTER 12

THE NEXT DAY, I looked at all my neighbors a bit differently. I couldn't help it. As luck would have it, on my way back from Met Food, I saw Miss Kirby herself. She was halfway up the block ahead of me, hunched over a shopping cart, wearing a Yankees cap. It was highly unusual to have a 'Miss Kirby out in the wild' sighting. I had only ever caught a quick glimpse of her beaky nose and beady eyes as I rushed past her door on my way up or down the stairs.

Her gait was lopsided and strained, her movement like that of a penguin. I watched her seeming to favor her right leg and bounce off her left as quickly as possible. I thought of her son who had died, of her living all alone in apartment 3D, and of the red bicycle with its sad streamers. Before I even had time to consider it, I was jogging up the sidewalk. I came up beside Miss Kirby, who swiveled her neck toward me with a startled expression on her face.

"Hello there," I said.

She gasped. "You shouldn't sneak up on people like that," she scolded. "It's rude!"

It was my first time standing face-to-face with her. From beneath the brim of the Yankees cap, I saw that same pointy nose that I recognized from the dark crevice behind door 3D. But she didn't look at all like a scary witch out in the noonday sun. Her body was small and seemed frail. A few stray, wiry, white hairs tumbled out from under the brim of her cap.

"I'm sorry I startled you," I said.

She clutched the handle of her shopping cart with white knuckles, as if she might be blown away by the slightest gust of wind if she hadn't had something to lean on.

"Well, what do you want?" Miss Kirby snapped. "You're not trying to sell me a candy bar or cookies or something, are you?"

"No, nothing like that," I replied. "Just wanted to see if you need help with bringing your groceries home."

Miss Kirby squinted up at me now. Her eyes were milky and unfocused, but suddenly a look of vague recognition registered, and she raised her brow.

"Ahhhh, …" she said. "You're Susan Casey's girl, right?"

"Yes," I answered.

"She was a bold one, too, just like you." Miss Kirby cackled, her face wrinkling up with a thousand deep lines and her mouth revealing several missing teeth. "The apple doesn't fall far from the tree, I see."

"I'm nothing like her, actually," I explained.

"A likely story," Miss Kirby said. But I noticed she loosened her grip on the handle of her cart, then slid her hand aside to make room for me. I gently reached over and grasped the cart and together we pushed it along. We didn't speak, just walked side by side, the groceries jostling in their bags as the cart's wheels bumped and jerked on the cracked sidewalk.

When we got to our building, Miss Kirby let me take her grocery bags out of the cart, which she folded up and carried in one hand, her other hand gripping the nicely polished stair railing as she slowly made her way up to the third floor. I followed behind her with the grocery bags, thinking, *How on earth would she have been able to do this alone? Several trips up and down the stairs, no doubt.*

Outside her apartment door, Miss Kirby leaned her folded cart against the wall and rooted through her ginormous beige pocketbook until she found her key. Then, with a shaking hand, she unlocked her door and pushed it open. The witch from the story of Hansel and Gretel flashed through my mind as I crossed the threshold with the Met Food bags, but I steeled my nerves and made my way inside.

Naturally, I expected apartment 3D to be laid out exactly the same as our apartment, so I was surprised to see that it was different and actually quite a bit larger. Rather than a long narrow hallway like ours upstairs, I stepped into a wide foyer. There were three bedroom doors instead of only two. While in apartment 4D, Grandma had her silly doilies and saint statues everywhere and the smell of cinnamon filled the air, Miss Kirby's home was dingy and drab, with shabby furniture and a sour, stale smell. In the kitchen, I placed her grocery bags on the countertop. When I turned around, Miss Kirby was holding out two crunchy dollar bills in her bony hand.

"For you," she said firmly.

I shook my head. "No, you don't need to pay me," I insisted. And I meant it.

A mere twelve hours earlier, my goal in life had been to fill that ladybug wallet with as many bills as possible and spend the money on a cross-country trip to find my father. I would've snatched up every dollar I could. But suddenly I didn't want Miss Kirby's money. I only desperately wanted to do something kind for her. Even if I wasn't sure exactly why.

"You'll take it," she said, raising her voice and shoving the bills into my hand. "To refuse is an insult to me."

I accepted the two dollars and stuffed them in my pocket, which earned me a gummy smile.

"Well and good," she said. "It's the least you could do for me. After all, you kids sound like a herd of rhinos living upstairs. It was nice and quiet around here before you showed up."

"It's my sister Judith who makes all the noise," I said. "I'm the quiet one."

Miss Kirby cocked her head and looked knowingly at me, just like the bird in the motel parking lot had those several weeks before.

"The quiet ones are the ones you really need to worry about," she said.

"Oh, you don't need to worry about me," I assured her. "I take care of myself."

She smiled and her eyes nearly disappeared in all the wrinkles. "I see," she replied.

As Miss Kirby walked me to the door of her apartment, I peeked into one of the bedrooms and saw a wall covered with lots of little colorful tiles put together to make a mural of flowers.

"Wow," I exclaimed. "How pretty."

Miss Kirby followed my gaze. "You must be looking at my mosaic art," she said. "I used to do that before my eyesight went bad, and then the arthritis in my hands got so severe that I couldn't even place the pieces anymore." She sighed.

"It must be hard," I said. "Not being able to do things you used to."

She nodded. "It is," she admitted. "That's why my pest of a niece is always trying to move me in with her. She's worried something might happen to me all alone here."

"But you don't want to move in with her?" I asked.

"Heck no!" Miss Kirby spat. "She and her husband are out in the boonies. I'd die of boredom."

I laughed. "The boonies really aren't so bad," I told her.

"Anyway," she said forcefully. "Like you, my dear, *I* take care of *myself*."

CHAPTER 13

FROM THAT DAY forward, it became a regular thing: every Tuesday and Friday, I helped Miss Kirby with her groceries. I had to keep myself busy while Rosa was downtown at her performing arts institute. Every day, I helped Grandma by keeping the apartment clean, and of course I also cared for the cats in the basement. I still hadn't worked up the guts to open storage locker #4D and peek in Mom's magenta suitcase. I told myself I would get to it soon; I was simply too busy with all the responsibilities I now had.

On the days I worked for Miss Kirby, we talked about all sorts of things. I confided in her about feeling like I didn't belong anywhere, since we had moved around so much after my dad left. She opened up to me about her life, too. She had come to New York as a young girl with her family, from Jamaica. She worked as a travel agent. She was a single parent. After her son Robin died, Miss Kirby became very sad. She made the mosaic mural in his old bedroom to honor him. Robin had loved flowers and being out in nature and riding his bicycle. Miss Kirby often spent time in his old room; it made her feel close to him, she said.

Miss Kirby gave me a dollar or two each time I helped with her grocery shopping or other errands and chores. But I didn't save all the money I earned in my ladybug wallet. I spent some of it on Italian ices from Nino's pizzeria for Judith and Dylan. Or on a buttered roll and a chocolate milk from Sanjar, the owner of the bodega on the corner. One afternoon when I was there, I saw James, the skater boy from 2C. He was buying an energy drink.

"What's up?" he said coolly when he saw me.

"Not much," I answered.

We walked out of the shop together.

"Goodbye, thank you," called Sanjar. We waved.

Outside, James dropped his board on the sidewalk and put one foot on it, but he didn't skate away. He opened his energy drink and took a giant swig. I turned to walk up the block.

"Where's Rosa?" he asked me. "I don't see you two together all the time anymore."

"She goes to a theatre program in Manhattan," I said.

"So, you went and replaced her with Miss Kirby?" He grinned mischievously.

"Hey," I said. "Have you been spying on me or something?"

James shrugged. "Naw. I just keep my eyes open about what's happening around the building, is all."

"Uh-huh," I said. *Is this flirting?* I wondered. *It feels like it might be flirting.*

I told James about how I had been helping Miss Kirby out.

"I'm impressed," he said. "Most people are scared of her and stay away."

"She's not scary once you get to know her," I explained.

James paused for a moment, looking at me with a strange expression that I couldn't read. His eyes were a deep, soft brown, and he had long lashes. "Most people stay away from me too. But here you are talking to me."

"Yeah, I guess I'm just weird," I responded.

We stood there looking at each other for what seemed like a full thirty seconds. Feeling awkward, I looked away first, fixing my gaze on a beam of sunlight breaking through the clouds overhead.

"It's gonna be a hot day," James said. "I'm going to the pool. Wanna come?"

"Pool?" I asked. "What pool?"

The summer was nearly over, and I didn't even know that there was a free public swimming pool just ten blocks away. I agreed to go, so James and I went to our apartments to get our swimsuits and towels, then met back on the front stoop.

As we were walking to the pool together, he pulled a vape pen out of his pocket and sucked on it, then offered it to me.

"Ew, no," I said.

He shrugged and inhaled again.

"That stuff is poison," I informed him.

"You've been hanging around good-girl Rosa Rodriguez too much. You won't tell on me like she did, will you?"

I shook my head. "No, go ahead and be stupid if you want to." I wanted to tell him I had seen all his stuffed animals down in the basement, but I kept it to myself.

"Hey," he said, "I heard a rumor that your dad is Iron Man. Is that true?"

"Maybe," I said, my tongue itching as the lie tumbled from my mouth.

"Doesn't he ever visit you?"

If only James knew how pointed that question was. It really stung.

"He's very busy working," I said curtly.

He nodded. "I bet. Anyway, you're lucky at least your mom's around," he said. "My folks both split on me."

I looked at him, confused. I thought he lived in apartment 2C with his mother. I had seen her leaving and returning from the building wearing a bus driver's uniform.

"Marie is my aunt," James explained, reading the question on my face. "She's fostering me because my parents are total screwups."

I didn't know what to say. Would it be rude to say "sorry"? I just said nothing. He continued.

"Everyone in the building hates me because my folks used to make a lot of trouble around here. People think I'm like them too."

"That's not fair," I responded.

"Tell me about it," James said. "Besides, I'm nothing like them."

No wonder people had warned me to stay away from James. They were prejudiced against him. I suddenly felt guilty for lying about my own father, and longed to tell James the truth. But I kept my mouth shut. I had made my bed already. No choice but to lie in it.

The pool was crowded and chaotic, not like the rec center in Middleton. We had to wait in line for half an hour just to get in. Once we were on the pool deck, there wasn't much room to spread out. There were no lockers, so we just had to leave our towels draped over the chain link fence. But the water was cool and felt good. It had been a long time since I had been in a pool, and I hadn't realized how much I missed it. I showed James how to do a few synchronized swimming moves: a back tuck, a water wheel, and an oyster. He wasn't any good, but I gave him good sport points for trying.

"I'm not all about this water dancing stuff," he joked, splashing me in the face.

I splashed him right back. "It's called synchro, not water dancing," I said. "And you should know it's an Olympic sport!"

"Well guess what?" James shouted, "So is skateboarding!" He splashed me even more, and I laughed and dove underwater to escape from the barrage. We stayed at the pool until closing, and the streetlights were already coming on by the time we walked back to Bainbridge Avenue.

That evening, I opened my top drawer and reached to the back to pull out my synchro ribbon. I looked at it and touched its gold lettering. First Place. I smiled.

Then Judith barged in, and I quickly tucked it away and shut the drawer.

"What was that?" she asked suspiciously.

"Nothing," I said.

She snorted. "*Someone's* got a lot of secrets."

"What's that supposed to mean?"

Judith smiled slyly. "Nothing. Just that I saw you with that skateboard boy earlier."

I threw a balled-up sock at her. "Get a life, Judith!"

She threw it back, teasing, "I was with my basketball team, and I saw you two walking past the Boys and Girls Club today. I never expected you to land such a cute boyfriend."

"Whatever," I said. "He's not my boyfriend."

But Judith didn't quit. "Did you make out with him?" she asked, eyes twinkling.

"What?" I shrieked, "No! Oh my God, shut up!"

Judith rolled her eyes. "See what I mean? Bo-ring!"

She pretended to yawn. I turned away so she couldn't see the blood rushing to my cheeks. James sure did smell good, and his eyes were definitely nice. Maybe getting my first kiss from him wouldn't be the worst thing in the world.

CHAPTER 14

MOM WAS HOME for dinner for a change. Vinny must've been on duty. Grandma had made homemade macaroni and cheese, and Dylan was so proud because he had helped. Dylan was becoming like Grandma's shadow. Those two were practically inseparable.

She took him to work at St. Brendan's with her during the week, and on Saturdays, he accompanied her to the laundromat to do the week's wash. Dylan considered himself quite the expert on fabric softener. On Wednesday nights, he stayed late at the church center for bingo, then afterwards he'd tag along with Grandma and her friends from the parish council to their weekly fellowship gathering at the diner on Webster Avenue. There, he drank chocolate milk through a straw while the ladies gossiped over cups of coffee and slices of pie, planning trips to Atlantic City and making suggestions for the theme of the next fundraising banquet. He had even picked up a new expression from them—"It takes all kinds"—which he used liberally. Grandma explained that it meant everyone belongs in God's house. It's not up to us to judge others, even if they seem strange to us.

"Dinnertime!" Dylan called now from the kitchen. "Get it while it's hot!"

"Where's Judith?" asked Mom, sitting down at the dinner table.

"She had a basketball game," said Grandma.

"They made the playoffs!" Dylan added.

Grandma bowed her head and said grace. Dylan said, "Amen," with gusto. Mom didn't say it, but she didn't roll her eyes either. She smiled instead.

"I guess you finally got your wish, Ma," she said to Grandma, scooping macaroni onto her fork. "You're converting Dylan, I see."

Dylan seized the opportunity to make an announcement. "Mom," he said, "if it's ok with you, I'd like to make my first Communion this weekend. I learned all my prayers, and Father Bannon says I'm ready."

"Dylan," Grandma scolded, "I was going to talk with your mother about that first, remember?"

I held my breath, ready for Mom to burst into a rant about the hypocrisy of the church. Instead, she dabbed the corner of her mouth with a folded paper towel.

"If it's really what you want to do, Dyl, I'm okay with it," Mom said.

"Really?" we all chorused.

Mom shrugged. "You know what? Who am I to tell people what to believe?" she said. "I don't have to go for Catholicism, but you can. It's a free country. We all need something to believe, I suppose."

Mom sure was less irritable than she used to be up in Middleton. Her relationship with Vinny and her job were both going well. She said her boss at work adored her because she had organized their office. This was the same woman who had never been able to locate our immunization records or birth certificates or school transcripts or any of that important stuff that most other moms, like Rosa's, probably kept stored safely in a neat file somewhere.

But for Perna Construction, Mom had suddenly become a rockstar. Of course, this could've all easily been a case of the *delusionals,* as Mom tended toward. But at least she was brushing her hair regularly, passing out on the sofa less, and smiling more. It wasn't the worst development in the world.

It wouldn't last, though. That much I was prepared for. As soon as Officer Delgado dumped her or cheated on her, she'd be back to the frumps again. I'd seen this movie before, multiple times.

"We light a candle for Grandpa Tom in the chapel every day," Dylan continued. "Right Grandma?"

Grandma looked at Mom and suddenly it was very quiet at the table. No one ever mentioned Grandpa Tom. There was an unspoken but clear understanding that the topic was a no-go zone.

Mom spoke first. "I didn't know you do that, Ma."

Grandma nodded. "We send a little prayer to him up in heaven, and ask him to watch over us all."

I noticed a shadow come over Mom's face. I wondered if, when she was my age, she missed her father, too, like I did. Did she think about him all the time, make up stories about him, wonder if he might've stayed, if only she were prettier, smarter, better at things?

Grandma asked, "Susan, do you remember those cute little porcelain statues that Daddy collected?"

Mom got up abruptly to clear her plate. "The birdies on the little knick-knack rack?" she said. "Of course, how could I forget? He loved those things."

"They were cute," Grandma said wistfully. "I wonder whatever happened to those. They just disappeared."

After dinner, I did the dishes with Grandma, then walked down the hall and saw Mom in the bathroom, doing her makeup in front of the mirror over the sink.

"You're going out again?" I asked her.

"Uh-huh."

The bathroom door was open, so I walked in and sat on the side of the tub.

"You really like Officer Delgado, huh?" I asked.

Mom smiled. "He's a great guy. And you should see his house in Pelham Bay, Vicki. It's huge. If things work out and we ever move there, you could have your own room." She batted her long eyelashes together, leaning in toward the mirror.

Classic Mom: jumping into talking about moving in with someone that Judith, Dylan and I have only met once for about five seconds. I didn't know where Pelham Bay was, and I didn't care.

She gestured toward her makeup bag. "Want to put some on?"

I shook my head.

"You sure?"

I nodded. Mom motioned for me to stand up. I did so and let her take my face in her hands.

"Hold your head still," she said. "Relax your eyelids and look up toward the ceiling." I felt the bristles of her mascara brush touch my eyelashes, and tried to suppress a reflexive flinch.

"Trust me," said Mom. "I promise I won't hurt you."

I willed myself to remain still. Mom worked on the lashes of my right eye.

"Hey, Mom?" I tried to sound casual.

"Hmmmm?" said Mom, moving over to the left eye with intense focus.

"You were eighteen when you met my dad, right?" I figured maybe she'd be open to the conversation, since we had just talked about her dad at dinner.

But she immediately stopped applying makeup and tensed up at the mere mention of him.

"Why do you ask?" she said defensively.

"I was just wondering, did you know him and Officer Delgado at the same time?"

Mom replaced the mascara wand in the bottle and screwed it in. She sighed.

"Blink a few times," she directed.

I obeyed. Mom looked through her makeup bag and pulled out a lip gloss.

"Put your lips like this." Mom puffed out her lips, and I imitated her.

She started applying gloss to my lips.

"It was like this, Vic," Mom said stiffly. "I went to prom with Vinnie, but I wasn't really his girlfriend. Back then I was looking for something more than a neighborhood guy. I wanted to *go places*." She let out a sarcastic little laugh. "I met your father downtown. He wasn't from the neighborhood. I thought he was my ticket out. Little did I know I'd end up right back here where I started." She held my chin up. "Wow. See how beautiful you look?"

Mom spun me around to face the mirror. In Mom's capable hands, a little mascara and lip gloss had transformed my face. I looked older. Glowy. Almost as pretty as Mom.

"Like it?" she asked.

"Yeah," I admitted.

In the mirror, my eyes met Mom's. She sighed.

"Vinnie's not your father, if that's what you're asking," she said.

"I wasn't—" I stammered. "That's not what I was asking!"

"I could see why you might think that." Mom continued, "Heck, I can see why you might *want* it to be true. But no. We never —y'know. *Did it*. Back then."

"Ew! Total TMI, Mom."

My face burned with embarrassment, so I looked down at the floor. In the trashcan under the sink, I saw the bottle of Mom's headache medicine. She followed my eyes to see where I was looking.

"Vinnie convinced me to flush the rest of those pills down the toilet," Mom said. "He showed me an article about them. Doctors prescribe them all the time, but they're too strong for what I need. And plus, they can be habit-forming. I don't need any more problems, I have enough already… as you well know."

I tried to hide my surprise and elation at hearing her talk sense.

She smiled. "Even your nutty mom can make a wise choice once in a blue moon," she said, giving me a little pinch on the cheek.

"Maybe it's the holy water working its magic."

She laughed. "Oh, okay, so Grandma's made a believer out of you, too?"

"Hardly," I snorted.

Mom picked her purse up from where it was sitting on top of the toilet seat and slung it over her shoulder. She was about to put her lip gloss into her purse, but handed it to me instead.

"You keep this," she said. "It's not my shade, and it looks gorgeous on you."

Then she kissed me on the top of my head and walked out the door.

CHAPTER 15

JAMES AND I hung out every day that week. He taught me how to do a kickflip on his skateboard, and I taught him how to properly do the oyster and a back tuck in the pool. Rosa made new friends downtown at the performing arts institute, but we still had our nightly chats in the airshaft. We even developed a special signal. In the dark, I would hear Rosa call, "Coo, coo!" and if Judith and Dylan were asleep, I would come to the window. Since she didn't have a phone like normal people, it was our special way to communicate.

She would tell me about her day, the songs she sang, the dances she learned, the roles she auditioned for, the funny or cool things her new friends said or did, and I would listen. I felt guilty knowing that Rosa confided in me while

I kept secrets from her. When she asked me what I was up to, I told her about helping Miss Kirby.

"She's an old witch," Rosa said. "Be careful."

"She's really not so bad, once you get to know her," I replied.

The truth is, Miss Kirby was actually quite interesting, kind, funny, and talented. It seemed people misjudged her because she was old, alone, and a bit afraid because she had trouble seeing and getting around.

Rosa went on, "I heard she's not the only one you've been hanging with."

"What do you mean?" I asked.

"My Papi has eyes and ears all over this block," she said. "What's up with you and James?"

I could sense the judgment in her question, and it annoyed me.

"Nothing to worry about," I said. "I need to have someone other than the cats to talk to while you're off with your actor friends. Is that okay with you?"

"It's your choice," she said. "Just watch your back. I care about you. I don't want you to get hurt, or ruin your reputation."

"Trust me," I said flatly. "I can take care of myself. More than you realize."

The words came out sharper than I intended. But I was tired of her being Miss Perfect and trying to tell me how to do things all the time. I could tell she was insulted.

"Listen," she said. "I wanted to tell you: I found homes for the cats. My friends Brianna and Emma are each going to take one. So, throw me down the key, will you? I'll make the exchange tomorrow morning."

I froze. I couldn't give back the key. Not when I hadn't even had the nerve to look in the 4D cage yet. My whole entire purpose, that I kept putting off. I quickly made up another lie.

"Shoot, I left it in my backpack out in the living room, and my mom's out there. I won't be able to get it without her becoming suspicious. Can I give it to you tomorrow morning? I'll meet you on the stoop early."

"I guess so," said Rosa.

We said goodnight and I went back to bed, trying to figure out what to do next. It was quiet in the room, with just the sound of my siblings breathing. Judith didn't grind her teeth anymore. She had won her basketball game and liked her friends at the Boys and Girls Club. She seemed happy. Dylan had changed, too. Mr. Choofie now resided in a place of honor atop the dresser. Dylan no longer felt the need to carry him around everywhere just to feel safe. They would both be fine once I was gone, I reasoned with myself. All the more space in the room for them after I left for California.

My phone lit up. It was James, texting me goodnight and asking if I wanted to go to the pool the next day.

I bit my lip, contemplating my next move. What I had to do was scary, important, and urgent. I needed moral support. James was someone whose family wasn't perfect. He didn't judge me like Rosa did.

I texted him back: "Can you meet me on the stoop in 10 minutes? I want to show you something. Top secret."

I waited. Then the three dots appeared, letting me know he was responding.

It was a thumbs-up.

The time on my phone said 11:55. The apartment was quiet. Mom and Grandma had gone to bed. I slipped on my sneakers and tiptoed toward the front door, dipping my finger in holy water as I passed. With each turn of the lock, the clicking sound seemed to ring out loudly in the dead night stillness. I held my breath. But no one woke.

It was strange to go down the staircase without hearing the usual sounds of life coming from neighbors' apartment doors. At that hour, the buzz of a fluorescent ceiling light was the only sound.

James was already out front when I got down there. He was in incognito mode with his hoodie pulled all the way up around his face. He was wearing basketball shorts and slides on his feet. There was an excited glimmer in his eye. I put my finger to my lips, grabbed his hand, and led him around the building, the way Rosa had done with me weeks before.

    I unlocked the green basement door. Felt along the wall for the light switch, and when I found it, the overhead bulbs flickered on. It was even spookier in the basement at night. With my heartbeat vibrating in my ears, we tiptoed in. This time, I went straight over to the #4D cage. I unlocked the gate and pushed it open. There was the magenta suitcase. It was time.

CHAPTER 16

"Woah!" James said, looking around the basement as soon as we descended the stairs. "This is sick. Are those my stuffed animals?"

"Maybe," I answered. "I'll open it up so you can see for yourself, on one condition."

"What is it?" he asked.

"Quit vaping," I said. "I like you. But I don't like that. And it's bad for you."

He looked at me. "You really like me, don't you?" he asked, flashing that cute, crooked smile.

"Don't get too full of yourself," I warned him. I opened up locker #2B and he picked up a plush Mario from the video game, hugging it like a long-lost friend.

"Awwww …" I teased.

"Shut up," he said.

"You can't tell anyone I brought you down here," I told him. "Rosa will murder me if she finds out."

He made a crisscross with his finger over his chest. "Promise," he said. And I believed him.

There wasn't any more time to waste. I went straight to apartment 4D's locker and used Ernesto's master key to open it up. James followed me. There before my eyes was the magenta suitcase, along with a few other bags that had been stuffed into the minivan when we left Middleton. It really didn't look like much, and it made me sad to see practically everything we owned sitting there on the concrete floor. James stood behind me, shifting awkwardly from one foot to the other.

"So, what exactly are we doing down here?" he asked. "I have a feeling you didn't bring me down here to reunite with my old toys."

I turned to face him, putting my hands on his shoulders. I took a deep breath and looked directly into his eyes. Maybe he thought I was about to kiss him. His eyes widened, his posture expectant. For a split second, I almost forgot what I was there for, and instinctively began leaning in towards him. He was close enough that I could feel his breath on my face. But my sense of urgency about facing what was inside locker 4D overrode whatever you want to call that funny feeling I was having for James.

"I have to tell you something, James," I said seriously.

"What?" he asked, clearly confused.

I winced. "For starters, my dad isn't really Iron Man."

"Yeah, I know that," he said.

"What?" I responded, shocked. "You already know?"

He nodded. "I've known for weeks. I googled him. After seeing you in Poe Park that day. That actor only has one kid. A son. And he's like, a grownup already."

I hung my head in shame.

"Why didn't you say anything?"

He shrugged. "I figured it was none of my business, and you probably had a reason for making that up. Besides, I didn't want to embarrass you."

I couldn't help it; I felt so grateful for his kindness that I gave him a hug.

"Thank you," I whispered.

He hugged me back. His embrace felt warm and safe. He smelled good, like soap and coconut.

"I'm sorry I lied," I said into his shoulder.

"It's okay," he said gently. "I understand."

I pulled away to face him again, then took another deep inhale, gathering the courage to be unflinchingly honest about who I was.

"See, the truth is my dad disappeared when I was a kid," I told him. "He ran off to California. For more than a year now I've been saving money to try to go find him. Because I can't believe he would actually just ditch and stop caring about us, y'know? Something must've happened to him. This probably isn't even making any sense to you. I'm sorry—"

James leaned toward me and pressed his lips to mine before I had a chance to even know what was happening. I closed my eyes. His lips were soft and sweet. My first kiss.

"I'll help you, Vicki," he said, after we separated. "What do you need me to do?"

We sat on the floor together, side by side, and I opened the latch of Mom's magenta suitcase. I was expecting to find information about my father, but what I found was stuff that my mom had kept about *her* father.

His U.S. Army discharge paper, his name in bold type at the top: **Tom Casey**. The photo of him in his uniform, a smaller version of the one I remembered seeing on Grandma's dresser all those years ago. A yellowing linen handkerchief wrapped around something small and hard. I unfolded it carefully to find a cream-colored porcelain dove statuette. Initially cool to the touch, the bird warmed quickly in my hand.

"My grandfather's knick-knacks," I said out loud, in awe. Mom had taken them.

James and I pulled out five more bird statuettes, each wrapped in a hanky.

A blue jay, a red robin, a yellow canary, a brown sparrow, and a plump little finch with an orange breast. He resembled the guy in the Middelton Motel parking lot to an uncanny degree. *You again*, I thought. *You seem to be following me everywhere. It can't be a coincidence. Nothing ever is.*

I lined up all the birds on the floor and looked carefully at them. They seemed to regard me right back with their painted eyes, as if they were real birds once, caught in the act of pecking or perching or chirping, frozen and immortalized. Fairytale birds, spirits trapped inside porcelain shells.

There I was bugging out on my grandfather's knickknacks, and I nearly forgot where I was and who I was with.

"Is this what you were looking for?" asked James, bringing me back to the present moment.

"Not exactly," I said. We wrapped up each bird again and placed them back into the suitcase with care. Except the finch. I put him in my pocket.

That wasn't all that was in Mom's magenta suitcase. In the zipper compartment was an envelope full of photographs. A school picture of Mom sat at the top of the pile. It looked like she was probably in seventh or eighth grade, with all her hair brushed to one side in a big poof. Her face in the picture was almost identical to mine. It was creepy, like looking into a mirror. The biggest difference between us is that her eyes were blue-green instead of gray-blue, like mine are.

"Woah, is that your mom?" asked James.

"Yeah," I said. "Weird, huh?"

"You two are twins," he said.

Another photo captured Mom as a teenager, all dressed up in a strapless dress, arms wrapped around a young man in a suit.

"Is that your dad?" asked James.

I looked closer, trying to recall what my father even looked like. The person I saw in my dreams about Ojai was enhanced by my imagination. It had been so long since he had disappeared, that to picture him, I had to conjure his grinning face in the apple orchard. All my own memories of him were nothing but fuzzy little snippets: meandering tunes he hummed in the car while his thumb tapped the steering wheel. The frayed fabric on the bill of his baseball cap. A curse word muttered under his breath as he shook his head in frustration about something I didn't understand.

But no, the young man in this picture in my hands wasn't my father. I looked closer and immediately realized who it was: a teenaged Officer Delgado. I recognized the bushy eyebrows and broad, confident smile. He had hair back then, and it looked funny, shaped like a helmet. He and Mom were posed on the front stoop, and Mom wore a big pink flower on her wrist. The night of their school dance. They looked happy.

There were also some weird things in the suitcase, odds and ends. Mom's I.D. badge from her last job upstate.

A bunch of concert ticket stubs. A schedule of my synchronized swim practices and meets from last year. A little strip from a fortune cookie with red print that said: *The fortune you seek is in another cookie.*

In other words, useless junk.

Except there was also an envelope addressed to Susan Hanlon, my mom, at one of our old addresses. Immediately when I saw it, my ears began to ring. The messy handwriting on the envelope and on the folded page inside was unmistakably my dad's. A long-tucked-away memory of his penmanship came flooding back into my mind: a song he was writing on the back of a green flyer advertising my preschool fundraiser, guitar balanced on his knee. Dad wrote like he'd flunked fourth grade. Not grown-up writing like Mom's and Grandma's. It looked worse than Dylan's chicken scratch.

I opened the envelope and took out the letter inside. As I unfolded it, I noticed the paper was crumpled, as if it had been balled up and tossed away, then fished out of the trash and flattened, handled many times over. I tried to focus on the words, but the tears in my eyes were blurring my vision.

Dear Susan,

Things can't go on the way they are. I've recently had a shift to realize my life's purpose: bringing light and awakening – I'm on another plane now, babe.

It's time to say goodbye. I'm honored you were part of my journey. I write to you today from my new home.

I never meant to hurt you and the kids. But we both know I couldn't ever be the husband and father you wanted or deserve.

Nothing but love,
Ryan

Tears stung my eyes. *Nothing but love?* What a crock. Dad hadn't called on my birthday, or Judith's or Dylan's. He didn't give a hoot when Mom lost her job, or when we got evicted. It was like he forgot all about us. And he was probably sitting on some pink mountaintop in California taking deep breaths and watching the sun rise, finding his inner *whatever. On another plane?* What did that even mean?

It was true, then. We were, in fact, disposable to him. What I simply hadn't been able to face all those years. My heart thudded dully in my chest. Why had I painted my mom as the bad guy in this story without any proof that she was lying? How badly I had wanted her to be wrong, to find that somewhere out there I had a dad like Ernesto, a solid guy who still loved us, but had just made a mistake and been cast away by our mean mother?

But no. It was me who was in the wrong. Mom was right all along.

I was despondent. James took the letter out of my hand and read it. Then he folded it up and put it back in the envelope. He stared down at it for a moment, then cleared his throat.

"I thought you said your dad took off to California," he said.

I sniffed and wiped my eyes dry with the sleeve of my sweatshirt.

"He did," I said. "And that's the proof! He's a total loser."

James showed me the envelope. "This postmark shows the letter was mailed from Queens, NY. Not California."

I looked for myself.

This is strange, I thought. *Some mix-up at the post office?*

I felt claustrophobic, like a trapped animal inside the metal storage cage. I heard my voice from somewhere far away utter a single word in confusion:

"Queens?"

I grabbed my phone. The cell reception was spotty in the basement, but within minutes I was able to learn there were fifteen Ryan Hanlons in New York, but only one in Queens. On 77th Avenue.

My head spun like the dryer in the laundromat. Was it really possible that Dad had been in the same state as us this entire time?

Suddenly, James and I were startled by a sound from above: a rapid knock on the door.

"Vicki, open up!"

It was Rosa's voice.

"I know you're down there. Open up NOW."

She didn't sound happy.

CHAPTER 17

I OPENED THE basement door and stood facing Rosa, putting my hands up in surrender.

"Busted!" I immediately called out, smiling awkwardly.

But Rosa wasn't smiling. She looked stern. She held her hand out and said only one word: "Key."

"I'm really sorry," I said, placing Ernesto's master key in her palm.

"You lied to me," she said. Her dark eyes showed me she was wounded. I could understand why. I had betrayed her trust. She pushed past me and walked down the stairs into the basement.

"Rosa," I said, trailing after her, "I was going to return it to you tomorrow, I swear. It's just that—"

She interrupted me. "My father could lose his job over this; don't you know that?"

"Oh God," I said. "No. I mean—I wasn't thinking, Rosa. I'm so stupid. Please, let me explain—"

It was then that Rosa caught sight of James, sitting cross-legged in unit #4D's storage cage, my mother's magenta suitcase open in front of him, and her things strewn out upon the floor.

Rosa put her hand on her hip and turned to face me once again, the disappointment in her eyes stabbing me like daggers.

"Oh, okay. I see what's going on here," she said, her tone cold as ice. "You *were* thinking, Vicki. Of yourself. The only person you seem to care about, come to think of it."

"That's not true," I protested.

"You pinkie promised that you wouldn't tell anyone my secret. And yet you bring *him* down here. Are the cats all right?"

"Yes, of course! And we can trust James, Rosa, I swear."

Rosa laughed sarcastically.

"I can't even trust *you*, Vicki," she said. "I must've been an idiot for thinking you were a real friend. Especially after I found out you lied to me about your mom being a court stenographer."

Cringe. "About that …" I began.

"Spare me," Rosa interrupted. "My cousin Alex does plumbing at Perna Construction. I saw your mom there. She's the temporary receptionist."

"I made up stories about my mother and my father because I was ashamed," I explained. "I'm sorry. I don't expect you to understand, because you have a mom and dad you can be proud of."

Rosa's eyes narrowed at me.

"I see," she came back. "Now it's somehow *my* fault that you're a liar?"

I looked down at the cracked concrete floor. Thought about license plates. Willed the tears to stay back.

"Rosa, at least let Vicki show you what she's just found," James said. "It's what she was looking for, the real reason she's down here. Then you'll see the truth."

Rosa followed me into storage cage #4D. I showed her what I had found, and told her the truth about my father. By then, I felt a tear on my cheek and angrily rubbed it away with my fist.

"I only lied because I wanted to impress you," I admitted.

Rosa didn't say anything for a moment, just looked from me, to James, to the magenta suitcase. She raised one eyebrow.

"That's crazy," she finally said. "You don't need to impress me. I'm your friend. You could've told me. I would've been there for you."

I wrapped my arms around her and gave her a hug. She hugged me back. This time it was me who might have squeezed just a bit too tight.

"So, what happens now?" asked James, when Rosa and I had finally pulled ourselves apart from our embrace.

For the first time in my life, I had complete clarity. My longing to reunite with my fantasy father was replaced with a new longing: to avenge the harm he had caused. Harm to Mom, to Judith, to Dylan, and to me. I still wanted to find him, but this time, to face him and let him see me. To tell him just how angry I was at him—not only for abandoning us, but for making me waste so much time dreaming about the version of him I wished existed.

"I'm going to Queens," I said firmly. "To confront him."

"Not alone, you're not," said James. "I'm coming with you."

"I'm coming too," said Rosa.

After we locked up the basement and returned to our apartments, Rosa and I finalized our plans in the airshaft. We agreed to meet on the stoop at eleven a.m. and go to the nearby subway station. We would take the train into Manhattan to drop off Angelica and Mr. Thing with their new owners, Rosa's friends from the performing arts academy. Then we'd venture on to Queens for my long-awaited reunion with one Mr. Ryan Hanlon. I wouldn't be alone. I'd be with my friends.

Two subway trains and a bus: not exactly a cross-country trip, but still an adventure. I said goodnight to Rosa, closed the window, got into bed, and texted James the plan. He responded with a thumbs-up.

And that's how it came to be that the next morning at exactly eleven a.m., when I ran down four flights of stairs and flung open the front door, there on the stoop was Rosa, her black hair shiny in two neat braids, and her big tote bag filled with a towel, two adorable cat heads sticking out the top of it. Beside her stood James, looking fierce, his hood up, trusty skateboard tucked under his arm. My heart fluttered. We were really doing this—together.

CHAPTER 18

THERE WAS A different item in each of the four pockets of my jean shorts that day, things I had placed there ceremoniously when I got dressed, feeling sure that I needed to have them with me on this journey.

In my back left pocket was the synchro ribbon, pretty much the only thing I'd ever won in my life. Back right pocket held my family apple picking picture—the way I wanted to remember the five of us together, realistic or not. In my front pockets, the little plastic Virgin Mary statue fit snugly on the right side, and my grandfather's sweet little porcelain lovebirds were tucked inside the left. My ladybug wallet was zipped up safely inside my backpack, along with the lip gloss Mom had let me keep. With these good luck charms, I felt prepared: a renegade ready for whatever the day threw at me.

Rosa, James, and I walked up the block together without saying a word, hoping our getaway wouldn't be delayed by a neighbor stopping to talk. The block was buzzing like any other Saturday morning. A delivery truck was parked outside the bodega. Sanjar, talking with the delivery man, put up his hand to give us a friendly wave as we crossed the street on our way to the subway station. The Doberman behind the chain link fence barked like crazy as we passed by. Luckily no one paid any mind to that dog, since he was always barking his head off.

After reading my father's letter the night before, I was more determined than ever to find him. Not for some childish idea of a happy reunion, like before—but to tell him off, face to face. To force him to see me. Maybe somewhere in my mind I still thought I could recreate that grinning family in the apple orchard, fit the pieces back together like the broken glass that made up the beautiful art of Miss Kirby's mosaic wall. But I told myself I had to toughen up and face facts: the mission had changed, and this encounter wouldn't involve any of the sunshine and palm trees I had dreamed about.

Once we arrived at the subway station, we descended the stairs. Down underneath the city, I inhaled the stuffy air, which strangely made me feel exhilarated.

Waiting for the train to come, James looked from me to Rosa and shook his head in disbelief.

"What?" I asked.

"If you'd told me a couple months ago that today I'd be standing on a train platform heading downtown with Rosa Rodriguez, teacher's pet and little miss perfect, I wouldn't have believed you."

Rosa scowled. "I'm not perfect," she said. "Where'd you get that dumb idea from?"

"From how, since second grade when I met you, every class you get an A-plus, you're every teacher's favorite, you never get in trouble or make mistakes," James answered.

"I do so make mistakes!" Rosa pushed back. "Excuse me for trying hard and applying myself, and not being a class clown, stoner, and all-around troublemaker."

I saw the hurt on James' face when he heard that, but he laughed it off.

"One thing I've realized," I said to them both, "is that nobody is just who they seem to be. You two may have known each other for years, but you've only seen a tiny part of one another. The other parts are hidden. And when you do actually get to know each other, you won't think those dumb things about each other anymore. Besides, the important thing is that now we've got each other's backs, right?"

Rosa and James looked at each other and nodded sheepishly. The lights of the approaching train shone on the tile wall as it screeched around the corner. It was time for the real journey to begin.

We sat together on the hard plastic seats of the subway car, the high-pitched sound of wheels on metal tracks ringing in our ears as we were carried along through the underground tunnel. A couple of young men wearing colorful clothes and bright white leather sneakers entered from the adjoining train car. They began an impromptu performance: one of them beat boxing while the other danced, spinning around on the floor and weaving in and out of standing passengers. When they were done, most people ignored them, acting like nothing had just happened. Rosa and I, unsure of subway train etiquette, applauded enthusiastically. I opened my bag, grabbed my ladybug wallet and pulled out a $5 bill, placing it in the can they held out as they walked through the car.

"Thanks darlin'," said the young man with a bright smile.

Rosa scolded me. "What are you doing? You should save your money."

I shook my head. "I earned it, and I get to spend it how I want."

"Suit yourself," said Rosa.

"I thought that performance was worth five bucks," James said supportively.

Giving the money away gave me a certain charge. I guess saving for California had been like a heavy weight I'd been carrying. Suddenly, I didn't have to hold onto it anymore. I wasn't going to Ojai, I was going to Queens, twelve miles away instead of three thousand.

The subway rumbled and picked up speed, rattling its way to our destination. Being jostled by the movement of the train was a rather pleasant feeling. A guy with tattoos sat to our left, listening to music in his earbuds and singing along, playing the air drums. Two older ladies wearing big, flowered hats sat to our right. And then there were Rosa, James, and me. Three kids no one paid attention to. With a destination no one knew. Just making our way somewhere.

When we came up from the subway we were on the island of Manhattan. It was my first time in the big city, and the energy of the streets there made Bainbridge Avenue seem sleepy in comparison. A lady with long pink hair stood in front of a clothing store handing out green flyers. She had rings through her nose, ears, and eyebrows. She handed me a flyer as I walked past. It was a coupon for 10% off my first tattoo.

"Thank you," I said. She didn't respond. In the garbage can on the corner, there were hundreds of green flyers. I threw mine in too, feeling a twinge of guilt for all that wasted paper.

A small crowd was gathered around a street performer with a cardboard sign saying "Billy Bellevue." We stopped to watch his routine. Billy put himself in a weird jacket with long sleeves and buckles that I had seen before in scary movies. He got someone in the audience to tie the sleeves behind his back and buckle him up tight. Then he picked another person to wrap a chain around his torso and legs, and padlock it.

Billy started gyrating methodically. He hopped up and down, then shook, looking as if he was spasming, grabbing leather straps with his teeth to unlatch them. After just a minute or so, he leapt out of his bonds, raising both arms triumphantly in the air. Everyone applauded. He passed around a hat.

It takes all kinds, I thought, remembering what Dylan and Grandma said about the parishioners at St. Brendan's. I dipped into my ladybug wallet again and put another five-dollar bill in Billy's hat. He smiled at me.

Mr. Thing meowed from Rosa's open tote bag.

"Ok, ok," I said, scratching the fur between his ears on the top of his cute little head. "We hear you. Let's get you to your new home."

"Which way is West 78th Street?" Rosa asked.

I pulled out my phone and looked at the map. So uncool.

"That way?" I guessed, turning in the middle of the sidewalk.

Someone bumped my shoulder as they were hurrying along.

"Watch it!" she growled.

Thankfully James knew his way around a little better than I did, because he had been downtown to skateboard a bunch of times. He guided us down the street, one right turn and two more blocks, folding us into throngs of people and pigeons and buildings and steam emanating from manholes and truck brakes whining and basement doors clanging open and shut. Past the smells of food carts, bus exhaust, pizza dough, and human beings in all their greatness and grossness. When we stopped, we were standing in front of a big, tall building with a green awning outside a grand entrance. A man in a uniform stood at the door.

James whistled through his teeth. "You didn't tell us your new friends were rich, Rosa," he said.

"We're here for Emma Dalton," Rosa told the doorman.

He nodded. "One moment please, Miss," he said.

He went inside the building, and Rosa and I looked at each other and mouthed the word 'Miss,' then started giggling.

The doorman made a call on a phone at a tall desk. After a moment, he gestured us inside.

"You may wait in the lobby," he said. "Miss Dalton will be down in a moment."

James, Rosa, and I sat on a fancy sofa that sat on a polished marble floor, with a huge floral arrangement on a table beside us. Two elevators with ornate gilded frames around them stood like stately soldiers guarding entry to the important people and places within.

"You can't tell who's rich at the performing arts institute," Rosa whispered, biting her nail. "Everyone seems the same there, you know?"

I put my arm around Rosa's shoulder. "I know this place is probably like super expensive or whatever, but to be honest, I like our building better," I said.

James agreed. "This one feels like a bank or something. Ours is much more welcoming. Thanks to your dad, Rosa."

"Awww, thank you guys." Rosa smiled and stopped biting her nails. The elevator dinged. Its doors opened and two beautiful girls stepped out. One of them wore her hair in long red, blue, and purple braids. The other was tall with blonde hair pulled back into a tight bun like a ballerina. When they saw Rosa, they squealed and started trotting toward her, arms outstretched.

"Rosa!" They hugged her, and then all three of them began doing choreographed dance moves in unison. James snickered, and I promptly swatted him.

"These are my talented friends, Emma and Brianna," Rosa said. "And these are my neighborhood friends, Vicki and James."

"No talent whatsoever," James said dryly.

"That's not what I meant!" shouted Rosa.

"Nice to meet you," I said to Emma and Brianna. I could see I had some tough competition when it came to being Rosa's bestie.

But they seemed nice enough, and they were thrilled to get their cats. It was decided that Emma would take Mr. Thing and Brianna would take Angelica. They promised that Rosa and I could come visit them any time we wanted.

I definitely felt a bit jealous because Rosa's friends were much prettier, richer, and cooler than I was; but James was looking at me, not them. And he winked at me again. I decided to be happy for Rosa that she had made friends with people who shared her interests. It was kind of nice to see this different side of her. The singing, dancing, goofier Rosa.

We left their fancy building where Rosa's rescued cats would live in the lap of luxury. The doorman tipped his cap to us and said, "Have a great day!" He probably lived somewhere more like our neighborhood. I wondered what pictures he might've had hanging on the walls of his apartment, and what secrets might've been stored in his storage lockers. I wondered if rich families like Emma and Brianna's had secrets and hidden things stored away as well.

Suddenly I felt very grateful to be walking up that wide sidewalk with James on my left side and Rosa on my right. I linked arms with them, and just like that, the three of us moved toward the subway station, past grand brownstones and buildings with shiny brass numbers and big buildings with funny cap-wearing doormen. Soon, we were back underground once again, this time pushing through the turnstile toward the Queens-bound side of the station.

CHAPTER 19

THE TRAIN TO Queens chugged out of the tunnel and took us high above the streets. It was a mesmerizing perspective. Even James and Rosa, who had lived in the city all their lives, had never been to the neighborhoods we passed through. We got off at the last stop and descended the station stairs. Street vendors with tarps laid on the sidewalks outside crowded shops were selling socks next to electronic toys next to baseball caps.

From there, we had to get a bus that would take us to the street where Ryan Hanlon had mailed the letter from. The bus took us through narrow streets lined with two-story attached houses with little concrete front yards. Some of them boasted Virgin Mary statues greeting passersby, magnified versions of the figure that was resting comfortably in my pocket.

James followed our route on his phone's maps app. He told me to press the yellow tape to indicate to the driver that we wanted to get off at the next stop. When the bus pulled away, we were standing on the corner of a quiet, residential street.

We walked in silence. When we got to the address we had for Ryan Hanlon, it was a modest little one-story red brick house with a broken treadmill in the front yard. An older woman sat on her front porch next door, looking us over.

"You lost?" the lady asked.

"No, ma'am," said Rosa. "Thank you."

I felt like my feet were stuck in quicksand, but Rosa and James pulled me up the walkway of the house. The neighbor lady on her porch watched us with suspicion.

On the doorstep, I began hearing a tinny ringing sound in my ears. For an instant, I completely forgot why I was there. I just knew I wanted to turn around and run. Rosa reached around me and rang the doorbell, then squeezed my shoulder. James held my hand.

After a moment, a lady came to the door, barefoot. She was drying her nails, which were painted purple. There was a TV on inside her house. It was loud, some movie or show with sirens and gunfire.

"Can I help you?" the lady asked. She blew on her fingernails. Her expression made it clear she wasn't in the mood for drop-in visitors.

I was unable to talk. My throat felt like sandpaper.

"Is Ryan Hanlon here?" asked Rosa.

The woman looked like she had just heard a dirty word. "No," she said slowly. "Who's asking?" She looked from Rosa to James to me.

I looked up at her and we locked eyes. Just stood there staring at each other for a moment. Then a strange, startled expression came over her face. She let out a little gasp.

Even absent the boots with bells on them, I recognized her. A memory came flooding back to me. She used to call me 'sweetheart' when she put the plate of waffles down in front of me at the diner upstate. Her face was droopier now, and the twinkle had left her eyes. But it was her, all right. The waitress. And all I could think of was *Wow. Mom was telling the truth.*

I was suddenly overcome with dizziness and nausea, and felt like I was about to faint.

The woman looked at her neighbor on the stoop next door.

"What're you starin' at, nosy?" she yelled. Then she stepped back inside her house and spoke to us through the screen door.

"I don't want any trouble with you," she said. "Your pop's not here. In fact, I'll be happy if I never hear the name 'Ryan Hanlon' for as long as I live. I ain't seen him in six years. He two-timed me, and left me high and dry."

I didn't know what that meant, but it didn't sound good. Probably the same thing he put Mom through.

"Do you know where he is now?" My voice cracked as I spoke.

The woman shook her head. "I swear to you, I don't." she said. "And the God's honest truth is I don't care where he is, neither."

I felt Rosa's gentle hand squeeze my shoulder again.

"She's been looking for her father for a long time," James explained.

The woman sighed. "I get it," she said to me. "But honey, if you was smart, you'd stop caring, like I did. Because Ryan Hanlon don't care about another soul on this earth except himself. That's the hard truth I learned about him. And I'm sorry I ever got involved with him, and I apologize to your mama too. You can take that to her from me. I was stupid. I feel bad that you was probably wishing to find your daddy here, and that he'd somehow be an alright guy or whatever. But I'm telling you: He just ain't."

There was deep sadness in her voice. I gulped and nodded. She blew on her nails again, and began to shut her door.

"Wait," I said.

She stopped and looked at me.

"Did you ever make it to California?" I asked. "With my dad? Ojai?" I had to know.

The woman gave a tragic little chuckle.

"Not even close. Ran outta gas in Pennsylvania," she said. "Then panhandled our way back here."

I nodded and turned around. I heard the door shut and click locked behind me. We were left standing on the doorstep. The whole exchange took less than three minutes. After years of my life imagining and plotting, it was devastating to have it go down like that.

I leaned on Rosa and James as we floated down the steps, back through the yard and toward the sidewalk. A blue jay landed on the handlebar of the broken treadmill and ruffled his feathers as if it was just another ordinary day.

All noises around me stopped. All movement slowed. My vision went fuzzy. I felt as if I was underwater, like when I used to be on the synchronized swim squad and the whole world was happening far away above the water's surface. All I had to do was focus intently on going with the flow: moving water with my arms and legs, controlling my breath, focusing.

But this wasn't a synchro routine. This was real life.

The nosy woman on the porch next door shifted in her chair, peered over, and shook her head disapprovingly. Rosa and James led me, despondent, up the block.

CHAPTER 20

On the bus ride back, I sat trying to catch my breath, trying to figure out if I was actually awake or merely dreaming. Rosa and James exchanged worried glances. Once on the train, it took us a few stops to realize we had missed our transfer and were going the wrong direction. So we got off at another station and walked upstairs, across, around a little maze-like tunnel, and back down another set of stairs until we were on the uptown platform toward the Bronx. I looked straight ahead at the window, where I saw nothing but darkness and my own distorted reflection.

I reached in my backpack and took out the lip gloss Mom had given me. My weird, delicate, embarrassing, but undeniably lovely mother – who maybe wasn't like the other mothers – but who had nonetheless managed to drag little shy, lonely, awkward me into all those scary first days at all those different schools I'd been to over the years; chatting up the ladies in the office as if it was no big deal, sweet-talking them into enrolling me even if she never had the right paperwork. And hadn't she been the one who signed the permission slip enabling me to join the synchronized swim squad in Middleton? And who had bought me a new dress from Target for my eighth-grade graduation? I opened up the lip gloss and put some on. Mom always told me I was beautiful, even when I felt like the ugliest girl in the world.

The naked realization hit me like a city bus: Mom had tried. Dad had lied.

I sat in that subway car and looked out the window as the train emerged from the tunnel and climbed in elevation. I saw the sky was getting dark and the lights in a million apartment windows were twinkling, illuminating the borough that had once been the boondocks where poets lived in little wooden cottages.

I started to cry. Not just a tear rolling down my cheek this time, but full-out sobbing. Next to me, James put his arm around my shoulder.

"Vicki? It's gonna be okay." There was sadness in his eyes.

"You're going home now," Rosa added, comforting me. "You have good family and friends on Bainbridge

Ave. who care about you. And anyway, California is some bullshit."

I had never heard Rosa curse before. It made me laugh, in spite of myself.

"How could I have been so stupid?" I said, putting my head in my hands.

"You're not stupid," James argued. "You just wanted things to be different."

"I'm useless," I said.

Rosa would have none of it. "No. You're amazing. Who else but you could make friends with Miss Kirby?" she asked. "No one ever thought *that* was possible."

James nodded. "And you brought the three of us together, too. You're special, Vicki, don't you see that?"

"Stop, you're embarrassing me." I wiped the tears from my cheek. "You said California was bullshit," I said to Rosa, half smiling.

James started laughing.

"Excuse my French," said Rosa. "I just wanted you to understand: we have a pretty good life right here, don't we?"

I nodded. She was right. And I realized something: I had never had best friends before. Real best friends. I had never before felt like I truly belonged.

"Thanks, guys," I said to Rosa and James.

It was a good thing the subway car was just about empty. The people who were seated in the car with us didn't even look up. I guess they were just used to people having breakdowns on the train.

The train doors opened at the next stop and two passengers walked in. One was a shabbily dressed woman carrying a shopping bag full of cans. The other was a man wearing a long coat and a stocking cap.

That's a strange outfit for such a warm summer day, is the random thought that immediately popped into my mind.

What happened next was a blur. The man in the long coat started walking toward us. The lady with the cans appeared to be about to sit down, and then, just as the man was about to approach the side of the car where we were seated, the woman dropped her shopping bag, sending cans clattering to the ground. She lunged toward the man.

"Stop! Police!" she yelled, tackling him and pressing him against a row of seats. He struggled, but she managed to get his arms behind his back and cuffed his wrists expertly.

Rosa and James and I looked at each other with horrified eyes. We didn't even have to say the words. We were thinking the same thing.

He'd been all over the news for two months. *Still at large.*

The subway flasher.

We screamed and ran to the other end of the car, tripping over empty cans that were now rolling around the floor. We held each other tight. The subway was now in between stations, speeding along the tracks.

"Don't be scared, kids," the woman called out. "I'm Officer Lee, undercover NYPD, and you are safe."

"Wow, okay, that just happened," I said.

"I can't believe she's actually a cop," said Rosa. "I'm in awe of her acting ability."

Officer Lee produced a police radio from inside her jacket. "Officer Lee to dispatch. Guess who I just got?"

At the next station, a slew of other police officers were waiting for them on the platform and took the subway flasher away. Officer Lee said she could arrange to have us driven home. Then I heard a familiar voice from behind me.

"I got this, Lee. These kids' families are worried sick about them."

We spun around to see Officer Delgado, looking sharp in his uniform.

"I've been in Queens looking for you all afternoon," he explained.

"How did you know we would be in Queens?" I asked, incredulous.

"Miss Kirby spilled the beans. Apparently, she heard you two talking in the airshaft last night. She gave us the info that you were headed to Queens, and I came out here to look. When I heard the report radioed in by Officer Lee and she said there were two girls in the subway car, I had a hunch it might be you."

"Sounds like you've had a heck of a day," said Officer Lee. "They're all yours, Delgado."

I was definitely ready to go home. And by home, I realized, I meant Bainbridge Avenue.

CHAPTER 21

The backseat of a police car was not a comfortable place to be. The seats were hard rubber. There were cages on the side and back windows, and a bulletproof plastic sheet separating me, James, and Rosa from Officer Delgado in the front seat. He slid it open so he could talk to us as he drove.

"Let this be the first and last time sitting in the backseat of a cop car for all three of you," he said sternly. "What were you kids thinking, anyway?"

Rosa and James both looked at me.

"It was my fault," I said. "Rosa and James were just trying to make sure nothing bad happened to me."

"You know you put you and your friends in danger by not telling anyone where you were going?" he said, raising one eyebrow at me in his rearview mirror.

"Yes, and I'm sorry," I said.

Officer Delgado didn't say anything for a few minutes after that. The sounds of the streets outside the window seemed like they were far away, in a different scene than the one playing out in the car. Rosa looked down at the hands folded tightly in her lap, and I saw that her cheeks were wet. James held my hand.

"Look. Don't get me wrong," Officer Delgado finally said, breaking the silence. "I get that being a kid ain't easy. You shoulda seen your mom and me when we were kids. We made our fair share of mistakes, too. The important thing is you learn from 'em."

We nodded in unison.

"I gotta say," Officer Delgado continued, "I can see you're a lot like your mom. Strong-willed like her. Determined. Resilient. I hope you know how lucky you are to have such an amazing mother. She's a fighter. Life will knock you down sometimes, but the winners keep getting back up again. That's what I think, anyway."

I looked out the window at the dark evening sky and the lights in all the windows in all the apartment buildings, blurring together as we drove down Mosholu Parkway.

Was Officer Delgado right? Was I lucky, after all? My pockets held my good luck charms for my big adventure that day. Silly superstitions. I knew they weren't magic. But were they …? The little Virgin Mary statue had brought me and Rosa together my first night on Bainbridge Avenue. And the lovebirds were entwined like my fingers were with James' in the back seat of that NYPD squad car. Or was it just my mind playing tricks again? I could probably manage to draw wacky connections with anything if I wanted to badly enough.

Officer Delgado turned the squad car onto Bainbridge Avenue and pulled to a stop right in front of our building. All eyes on the block were on us. Teenagers on the stoops turned and looked, and neighbors peered out their front windows. Shoppers came out of the bodega. And there we were in the back seat, where the criminals usually sit.

"This is gonna give you some major street cred," said Officer Delgado, his tone suddenly jovial. "Act tough when you get out of the car. Give 'em a mean glare. Nobody will mess with you ever again." He chuckled to himself.

By the time Officer Delgado let us out of the back, a small crowd had gathered on the sidewalk in front of the building.

"What'd they do?" someone shouted.

"That boy is up to no good," another neighbor said, looking sideways at James.

"Just like his folks," someone else commented. "Apple doesn't fall far …"

I squeezed James' hand. I could tell from the way he hunched his shoulders that he had heard the nasty comment.

"Nothing to see here, folks!" yelled Officer Delgado. "Shoo now!"

He escorted us to the front stoop. Ernesto and Arcelia rushed out, looking upset.

"Rosa!" shouted Arcelia. "Thank God you're safe!"

"I'm sorry I worried you," Rosa said. She ran up to them, and they all embraced.

"Don't be too hard on her," Officer Delgado said to Ernesto. "These three have had a long day. I think they've learned a lesson or two."

Rosa disappeared into 1A with her mother and father. James gave me a hug and then went with his Aunt Marie into 1C. Officer Delgado walked me up to the fourth floor. Before he even had a chance to knock on the door to apartment 4D, Dylan ran out and gave me a big hug, clinging to me in a way that made me feel very ashamed for leaving him behind.

"I thought you went away forever and were never coming back," he sobbed. "Like Daddy."

I hugged him tight and stroked his head. "I'll never do that," I said. "I promise."

Judith joined in the hug too.

"Don't freak us out like that again, please," she begged me.

"I won't, Judith. I'm so sorry."

Grandma approached the door, and Mom stood at the far end of the hallway. She looked so small and tired and faraway.

"You and your mother should probably have a talk," Officer Delgado said to me. "What do you think?"

I nodded. Officer Delgado turned to Grandma. "Mrs. Casey, how about I take you, Judith, and Dylan across the street for Italian ices?"

CHAPTER 22

I WALKED SLOWLY down the hallway to where Mom stood. She pointed at the sofa. At one end in a neat stack were the pillow and blanket she used when she slept there every night.

"Sit," she ordered.

I did as I was told, for once. The sofa was lumpy. No wonder Mom looked tired sometimes. It couldn't have been a very comfortable place to sleep.

She sat down next to me and stared at her knees. "I can't believe you went there," she said.

"I'm sorry if I worried you, Mom," I said.

"I wasn't worried," she said. "I was surprised."

"I don't get it, Mom," I said to her. "Ernesto and Arcelia were worried about Rosa, and Marie was worried about James. How come you weren't worried about me?"

"Because I know you're strong, you're smart, and you've got a good head on your shoulders," she said. "You're not stupid like I was at your age."

Mom had never called me smart before.

"I'm not *that* smart," I insisted, cringing to think about how close I'd come to taking a train across the country all by myself, to a place where I didn't know a soul.

Mom turned to face me. "Look, I get it, Vic," she said. "You were curious about your dad. You tried to ask me about him plenty of times before. I know I should've been more open with you. I just ... I guess I thought it'd be easier if we could all just forget about him and move on."

I shook my head. "I think about him all the time," I confessed.

Mom let out a heavy sigh and took my hand in hers.

"I'm sorry, Vic," she said quietly. "Of course you do. It's only natural."

"I really wanted to think my dad was a good guy," I told her. "But obviously, he *really* wasn't."

Mom thought for a second, then cleared her throat. "Nothing's ever black or white. All good or all bad. It would be simpler if things were like that, but they just aren't. Your dad and I had some good times together. I ran away with him because I was searching for something I didn't know how to find on my own. It didn't turn out the way I'd hoped. But if I hadn't met Ryan, then I wouldn't have you, Judith, and Dylan. And you three are what's kept me sane all this time. That's the truth. So, in a way, I'm grateful to him. For that."

A tear ran down my mother's face. Instinctively, I reached over and wiped it away.

"Would you believe I once thought I had it all figured out?" Mom chuckled. "Wow, I sure did mess things up, didn't I?"

I shook my head.

"No, Mom," I said. "You didn't. You held us together somehow. And you brought us here. We like it here. We're good."

Mom took my face in her hands and looked me straight in the eye. "Vicki, I want you to hear me say something: The stupidest thing I ever did was believe a man could whisk me away from reality and give me a fantasy life."

All the fantasies I had created about a life in Ojai danced around my brain.

"I have his genes, Mom," I said. "Does that mean I'm going to be a screwup, too?"

"No way!" she said. "We all make mistakes. But we don't have to be like our parents."

I supposed she was right. Look at James, and how frustrating it was that people kept thinking of his parents when they saw him. He was determined to forge his own path, much different from theirs. If he could do it, I could too.

"My father had his problems too," Mom continued. "Believe me, I get it."

"You and Grandma never talk about Grandpa Tom," I ventured. "But ... I found a picture of him ... in the basement."

Mom looked out the window. She didn't ask what I'd been doing in the basement. A pigeon fluttered down and perched on the sill outside.

"I didn't know my father too well, I'm afraid," she said, looking at the pigeon instead of at me. "Grandma used to say he was different before the war. But I only remember him after he returned. He'd be there in the room, but his mind was always somewhere else. He would drift away, like he wanted to escape his own thoughts. He never spoke about his experiences at war. To be honest, in our household, we never spoke about much of anything."

"That tracks," I said.

Mom frowned and rubbed her forehead. "After a while, he started going out, staying out late into the night. Then disappearing for days. Then longer. Grandma would go out looking for him, drag him back home. And I'd be all alone in the house, scared. The last time she went looking, she couldn't find him, and he didn't come home at all."

"That sounds strangely familiar ..." I said.

Mom turned from the window and looked back at me. "I didn't mean to repeat the pattern, Vic," she said. "I genuinely thought I was breaking away." She offered a sad little half-smile. "Major fail."

"Did you ever find out what happened to Grandpa Tom?" I asked.

Mom looked up at the ceiling and pursed her lips together. I could tell it was hard for her to get the words out.

"It was suicide. Which is considered a sin by the Catholic Church. And you know how Grandma is about that stuff. We simply never talked about what had really happened. Like it was a curse. A big, ugly, tragic, secret curse that ate away at us."

Poor Mom. Poor Grandma.

"You locked your secrets up inside and threw away the key," I said.

"Yes," Mom agreed.

I felt a dull pang in my heart, thinking about the young soldier in the photograph downstairs. Thinking about my dad at the apple orchard with his silly grin. And Mom's school picture, with her poofy hair.

"This all explains a lot," I whispered.

"I'm sorry you were never allowed to talk about your feelings about your father," Mom said. "I should've done better. I will do better, from now on, okay?"

She tousled my hair and looked at me as if seeing me for the first time. "You're different from me though, Vic. You're stronger. Promise me you'll believe in yourself, and not depend on someone else to save you. Okay? Will you promise me that?"

I curled my pinky around my mom's.

"Pinky promise," I said.

She smiled. There were little lines around her eyes. Crow's feet, I think they're called. But her eyes were so clear and a beautiful deep blue. Not foggy like when she used to take those pills. Officer Delgado had helped her get rid of those. Maybe he really did care about her.

The pigeon on the windowsill outside ruffled its feathers and cocked its head, peering in at us.

"Looks like we've got an audience," said Mom.

"Oh, yeah. Birds follow me sometimes," I said to Mom. "I think they might be looking out for me."

Mom shrugged. "I guess anything's possible." She pulled a strand of my hair out of my face and tucked it behind my ear. "How'd you get to be so smart and thoughtful and brave, anyway?"

"Miss Kirby and Officer Delgado both say I take after you."

Mom laughed through her tears. "Let's hope not. For your sake."

I took a deep breath. "I made you a promise. Now you have to make me one, Mom."

Mom looked at me squarely. "I'll try. What is it?"

"Promise we will *not* move in with Officer Delgado to his house in Pelham Bay. At least not right away."

"Why? Don't you like him? And wouldn't you like your own room? Some privacy?"

"I *do* like him, and it'd be amazing to have my own room again. But … you don't have to rush your relationship for me," I said. "Plus, I don't want to leave Bainbridge Avenue. I don't want to leave Grandma, or my friends. For the first time in my life, I feel like I belong somewhere."

Mom stood up and walked to the window overlooking Bainbridge Avenue. The pigeon boldly preened itself, unbothered by her closeness.

"Wow," she said. "Can you believe I lived here most of my life and never appreciated it until right this second?"

Her silhouette was illuminated by the streetlights below. I followed her gaze. It *was* hard to believe. Because it was beautiful.

Once upon a time, my mom tried running away from here with my dad, and she ended up back again. Maybe—finally—it was time to stop running.

CHAPTER 23

Officer Delgado brought back a small pizza from Nino's for me and Mom to eat. It was fresh out of the oven. Hot, savory, delicious, bready, and cheesy comfort.

While we ate our slices, Dylan modeled his first Communion outfit for us: an all-white suit, including a white clip-on tie and white loafers. Mom said he looked like a disco dancer. Grandma said he looked like an angel. Judith said he looked like a marshmallow. I said he looked like a dove. He smiled, beaming and accepting each as a compliment. Nothing could interfere with his pride.

The next morning, Mom told me I needed to apologize to Arcelia and Ernesto for making them worry about Rosa. She brought me downstairs and knocked on the door of apartment 1A.

Ernesto opened the door wide and invited us in. Rosa was washing dishes at the kitchen sink. Arcelia called to her and she came out, wiping her hands on a dishtowel. When she saw me, she ran up and gave me a big hug.

"I'm very sorry for running off and bringing Rosa without telling anyone where we were going," I said. Arcelia and Ernesto each gave me a hug.

"We live and we learn," said Ernesto. "It's what life is all about."

"And loving your neighbor," added Arcelia. "We all must look out for each other, *sí*?"

"*Sí*," I agreed.

"I have some business to do with Ernesto," Mom declared. "Vicki, why don't you and Rosa go hang out in her room for a while?"

"What business?" I asked.

"Grown-up matters," she said.

What was going on here?

Arcelia smiled. "I will bring you a snack," she said, shooing us down the hall toward Rosa's bedroom.

Later that day, Ernesto brought the magenta suitcase up from the basement, at Mom's request. She, Grandma, Judith, Dylan, and I all sat in the living room and went through it together. Mom and Grandma sat on the sofa with the suitcase open on the coffee table in front of them,

Judith and Dylan were cross-legged on the floor, and I stood, watching their reactions.

Mom shuddered when she saw the picture of Grandpa Tom wearing his army uniform.

"He didn't mean to hurt us," Grandma whispered.

"I know," said Mom softly.

"Is that our grandfather?" asked Judith, her eyes wet. Mom nodded.

"My grandfather looks brave," said Dylan, peering over Grandma's shoulder.

"I suppose he tried to be," Grandma replied.

I stepped away, went to the kitchen, and brewed a pot of tea the way Grandma had taught me. Judith came in, and without saying a word, set out cookies onto a plate. We put the tea and cookies on a tray and stood back to inspect our work. Judith and I smiled at each other, because we both knew the presentation was perfect. We had come a long way from the feral kids we'd been when we'd first appeared at Grandma's door that day we arrived.

I proudly carried the tray back to the living room, with Judith at my side. The mood had changed considerably. Mom and Grandma were now laughing at the prom photo picturing young Mom and Officer Delgado posed on the front stoop.

"That's a framer, for sure," cackled Grandma.

"Christ. My hair," Mom laughed. "I don't remember it being so awful."

"You used a whole can of hairspray that night," Grandma remembered.

"Now we know who to blame for the hole in the ozone layer," Judith remarked.

Mom laughed. Then Grandma spied the porcelain birds wrapped in handkerchiefs.

"How Tom loved those little statues!" she said wistfully. "I thought I'd never lay eyes on them again."

"I'm sorry I took them when I moved out all those years ago, Ma," said Mom to Grandma. "I just wanted something to remember him by."

"It's okay," Grandma replied. "I understand." She held the blue jay in her hand. "Tommy bought this little guy at a shop in Rockaway Beach." She then proceeded to pick each one up in turn. "This one on a summer vacation in the Adirondack Mountains, this one I think was from a mail-order catalog."

"What about this one?" I asked, producing the lovebirds from my pocket.

Grandma clapped her hands together. "That's the best one of all," she said. "The lovebirds. I bought it as a birthday present for him ... And I think your grandfather would want you to have it, Victoria."

I looked at Mom. She nodded in agreement.

CHAPTER 24

Twenty children dressed in white lined up on 207th Street in front of the entrance to St. Brendan's Church that Sunday. They looked like a gaggle of little geese, all fidgety and nervous and excited and itchy from lace and polyester.

"We'll see you in there, Dyl," called Mom, all dressed up for the occasion. I noticed that Officer Delgado, wearing a sharp suit and tie, could barely take his eyes off her.

"You got this, kiddo," Officer Delgado said to Dylan, giving him a fist-bump.

Inside, the church was packed with families, phones poised to take videos as soon as the kids began their procession in the door and down the aisle. We took our seats in a pew toward the front of the church. Organ music started and the line of children entered, walking slowly and ceremoniously. Dylan kept his eyes straight ahead, his chest puffed out, his chin up, and his hands in prayer, showing off the serious, oh-so-holy stride he'd been practicing over and over in the hallway of the apartment. But he couldn't help grinning proudly as he passed by Grandma. I tried to remain pious but couldn't stop myself from smiling, either.

At the altar, when it was his turn, Dylan bowed to the priest as he held up a Communion wafer. I felt a strange respect for my brother in that moment. He had gone and done something he really wanted that made him feel safe and good.

After the priest placed the wafer in Dylan's little outstretched hands, instead of putting it in his mouth like the other kids, Dylan carried the holy host back to the pew with him, holding it up to show it off, as if it were an Olympic medal.

"Oh, dear Lord, no," Grandma groaned, embarrassed. She covered her face with her hand. We all giggled as silently as we could.

After the service, we walked out the front doors of the church and posed for photos with Dylan on the sidewalk. He announced that the wafer tasted like cardboard, but in a good way.

We walked through Poe Park on our way home. Officer Delgado hoisted Dylan up on his shoulder and we all sang "For He's a Jolly Good Fellow."

"Say cheese!" I shouted. I managed to fit everyone in the frame and snapped a selfie with my phone. Then the others walked on, and I stood frozen for a moment underneath a lovely elm tree right next to the raven-shaped visitor center. I looked at the picture I had captured—all smiling faces. The moment felt almost too perfect, to the point where it frightened me terribly.

I couldn't let this shot become another image of fleeting happiness, like the photo in the apple orchard. I wanted it to last this time.

Gripped by panic, I deleted the photo and ran to catch up with my family.

When we arrived at our building, Rosa and James were sitting on the stoop.

"Something special is happening today," Rosa sang as we approached.

"Yup," I responded. "Dylan's first Communion."

"That's not what she meant," snickered James.

"What's going on?" I asked. I slapped James playfully on the shoulder. "C'mon. You know I don't like secrets."

"You'll like this one, I promise," he said, smiling in a shy way that I could not help but find adorable.

I didn't have to wait long to learn what the secret was. Mom made an announcement.

"I have some exciting news to share with everyone," she said. "First of all, I'm officially a full-time employee of the construction company."

We all applauded.

"I even got my insurance cards," she said. "We can all go get our teeth cleaned!"

She held two little plastic cards up, waving them as if they were winning Lotto tickets.

"Mom," Judith laughed, "you definitely over-hyped this news. Dentist visits are not very exciting."

"But that's not all," Mom said with a twinkle in her eye. "Follow me."

She led us all inside the building and up the stairs. It was like a funny little parade: Mom leading the way, followed by me, Grandma, Judith, Dylan, Rosa, James, and Mr. and Mrs. Rodriguez. But instead of going all the way up to our apartment, we stopped on the third floor. Mom knocked on Mrs. Kirby's door.

"Is Miss Kirby alright?" I asked, worried.

My question was answered when the door opened and I saw Miss Kirby smiling, her face a million creases. Whatever this surprise was, she was definitely down with it.

"How long have you been eavesdropping on me and Rosa in the airshaft?" I asked her.

She laughed like a funny old crow. "Since the very first night with the little plastic Saint Mary," she said, with a wink.

"You're a rascal," I told her, laughing.

"Takes one to know one!" she shot back playfully. "Come in, come in."

We followed her inside her apartment. There were boxes stacked in the living room.

"What's all this?" I gasped. "You're not moving, are you, Miss Kirby?"

She patted me on the arm. "There, there, dear. It's okay. My niece is taking me to live with her on Long Island."

"The boonies?" I exclaimed. "You hate it there!"

She chuckled. "No dear, I was just afraid of change. But it's time. I'll have a lovely view of a tree out my window. The birds will come sing me awake every morning. Change can be scary, but it can also be very good. Getting to know you has taught me that."

She reached out a hand to me, and I held it. Then she let go and turned around to her giant pocketbook that was sitting on an armchair. She rooted through it for a moment, then turned around and presented Mom with a ring of keys.

"It's all yours, Susan. Take good care of the place." Her milky eyes gazed around the room. "It's time for me to move on."

"Wait, what's happening?" I asked, confused.

Mom looked at me. "The apartment is ours!" she exclaimed, beaming. "I already gave Ernesto the security deposit and signed the lease."

Miss Kirby smiled. "You may need to patch up the broom handle marks on the ceiling."

Judith, Dylan, and I looked at each other, speechless.

Rosa clapped her hands together gleefully.

"You're one floor closer to me now!" she cried.

Dylan rushed over to Miss Kirby and gave her a hug.

"I'm sorry we thought you were a witch," he said. Everyone laughed, including Miss Kirby.

"So am I," said Judith, adding, "but we can come visit you on Long Island if you like."

"Offer accepted!" said Miss Kirby. "But only if you bring me some Nino's pizza."

"Deal," I said, nodding.

"Oh!" said Miss Kirby, "I almost forgot …" She disappeared behind one of the large boxes and emerged with the red bicycle that I had seen down in her storage area. She wheeled it over to Dylan.

"I thought you could make use of this," she said to him. "It was my son's and he loved it. They don't make 'em like this anymore. It just needs a little tune-up to be good as new. A Communion gift."

Dylan's eyes filled up with tears of happiness.

"I love it, thank you!" he exclaimed.

"Mom, does this mean I can have my own room again?" I asked hopefully.

She shook her head. "Sorry, kiddo. You'll share with Judith. Dylan will have his own, since he's the only boy, and finally—I'll have my own, too!"

Judith gave Dylan a pinch. "Little Prince," she teased.

"At least you don't grind your teeth anymore," I said to Judith. "And you deserve your own space, Mom." She smiled and put her arm around me.

As the movers carried Miss Kirby's things downstairs, we walked from room to room. This was going to be our very own apartment. I would still be on the airshaft, just one floor below our old room, in Robin's old room, with the beautiful mosaic mural on the wall. With Grandma right upstairs, and James and Rosa downstairs. I couldn't believe my luck.

CHAPTER 25

Ernesto made apartment 3D look as good as new. He applied a fresh coat of paint and patched up the broom handle marks on the ceiling. I did a full inspection and couldn't find any ancient hairs stuck in the crown molding, which boded very well indeed.

In my new room, I loved running my hand over the smooth glass and stone pieces of the mosaic. Miss Kirby's art burst to life—taking shape in flower petals, grass, and sky; a glorious scene made of thousands of tiny pieces of broken fragments that had been put back together to create something magical. I loved it even more knowing that Miss Kirby had made it all by herself, for her lost child. Nobody in the building had really known who she was or what she had gone through, or what beauty came out of her lonely heart that was full of pain and longing.

Rosa spent more and more time with Emma and Brianna in Manhattan. But, every night we'd still meet up to talk to one another in the airshaft, even though Ernesto and Arcelia finally got her her own phone so that in the future, if she went anywhere, they'd be able to reach her. Still, we both agreed that our chats in the airshaft were better than texting.

Grandpa Tom's porcelain lovebirds sat perched on top of my new dresser that Mom had scored at Goodwill. My ladybug wallet, synchro ribbon, Virgin Mary figurine, and lip gloss were still stored in the back of my top drawer, along with the picture from the apple orchard.

Dad's smile looked real in that picture. Could it have been possible that he'd been truly happy with us in that moment? Was he completely lying even back then, on my eighth birthday? Or maybe, was he in some strange way ... *trying*? It hurt to think he might not have ever cared about me. But I still didn't believe that was entirely true. Maybe I'd never know for sure.

I sometimes took the picture out and studied it for a minute or two. The wondering about him didn't stop. But the fantasizing and scheming did.

My family wasn't the only one with secrets. I had at least learned that, by then. James was secretly a stuffed animal collector. Miss Kirby was secretly an artist with a broken heart. Rosa was a secret rebel, Mom and Grandma had a secret pain, and I'd had a secret plan. My dad probably had the most secrets of all. Ones that I may never know.

That day at the apple orchard when the picture was taken, things were certainly not what they seemed. But people are more than their secrets. Way more.

On my phone, I opened my deleted photos folder and looked at the one I had taken at Poe Park on our walk back from Dylan's first Communion. It still scared me to look at it, to hope that things would work out and we'd get our happily ever after. But even stronger than my fears was my hope, and I decided I didn't want to lose the picture of that hopeful moment. I moved it from the trash into my hidden folder. Some things remain too precious not to be protected and kept secret. At least for a while.

I went to my airshaft window, opened the screen, and peered down at the dingy ground at the bottom. Then I looked upward at the octagonal patch of sky overhead. Pigeons cooed and fluttered on the rooftop, carrying on with their own lives. On a telephone line outside, there suddenly landed a chubby little bird with an orange breast. I couldn't believe my eyes. Impossible! Bainbridge Avenue was strictly pigeon territory. But there it was! It peered in at me, and then, as if satisfied with what it saw, flew away.

Maybe one day I too would spread my wings and explore the world, I mused. Maybe even see California, and those palm trees I'd dreamed about. But for the time being, I felt just fine being right at home on Bainbridge Avenue. Where I belonged.

ACKNOWLEDGMENTS

BIG THANKS GO to my whole family, especially my sister, Liz, who used to play Rose-Vic with me and who originally gave me the idea to write down this story. I'm indebted to my mother, Kate, who lived on Bainbridge Avenue and was known to occasionally enjoy a pickle and a bag of chips on the front stoop. Also, I'm grateful to my talented daughter, Riona, who read an early draft of my manuscript and gave me invaluable insights from a real live teenager. I'm lucky to have a fantastically supportive husband, Jason, who always clears the way for me to write. Big shout out to my brother Roy, who back in the day was even smarter, sweeter, funnier, and more resilient than Vicki's little brother Dylan, and who was the first published author in the family (together with his talented wife and co-author, Sarah). My sons Harley and Ray inspire me daily with their magic mix of confidence, courage and compassion, and they always cheer me on. And finally, I would like to acknowledge my father, Geoff, who unlike Vicki's dad, never disappeared, always could be counted on to pick up the phone, and never gave up on his dreams.

My appreciation also extends to the L.A. NaNoWriMo "Working Title" crew—especially Julie Johnson, Nina Prasad, Kit Russell, and Jennifer Wang—who first helped me form this story into something resembling a novel; to Wendy Rohm and my Dublin and San Diego writers retreat pals for unending encouragement, creative ideas, and good times; and to Victoria Abril, Lizzy Pierson, and Felipe Ossa for being excellent beta readers. Two additional rockstars I'd like to thank are Nazrin Choudhury and David Zellnik—both exceptional writers themselves. I'm grateful for the lovely weekend I spent glamping in an airstream trailer in Cape Cod with Nazrin, whose energy and drive are infectious; and for the times spent reconnecting with David over wine in Hell's Kitchen or sangria in SoCal; what a gift to have a friend who's an insightful listener and a brilliant story doctor. Without the support of all these wonderful people, I wouldn't have gotten this book over the finish line.

ABOUT THE AUTHOR

Norah Lally was born in New York City and cherishes many fond childhood memories spent in her grandmother's neighborhood in the Bronx. *Back to Bainbridge* is her first novel. She has numerous screenwriting credits, including the KidsFirst! Award-winning short film Danger Jane, PBS Kids' It's a Big, Big World, and MTV's Celebrity Deathmatch, which she co-wrote with her BFF and former writing partner, Meg Ables. Norah currently resides in Los Angeles with her husband, children, and the family Shih Tzu, Murphy.

www.ingramcontent.com/pod-product-compliance
Lightning Source LLC
Chambersburg PA
CBHW032041200426
43209CB00078B/1968/J